They said she could never come back. Now she's #1.
Here is the most inspiring story in professional sports,
featuring:

- Monica Seles' amazing beginnings as a true tennis
  prodigy, without any formal training, at seven years
  old.

- How Monica became the youngest player ever to be
  ranked #1—in March 1991—aged seventeen years,
  three months.

- The tremendous support of her family: from her
  father's lessons to her entire family's odyssey to the
  United States.

- Her terrible tragedy at a 1993 tournament in Germany, at the hands of a deranged tennis fan.

- The amazing comeback in the 1995 season, and the
  dramatic U.S. Open where she was undefeated until
  losing to Steffi Graf in the final round.

- Her stunning 1996 victory at the Australian Open—
  her first grand-slam championship victory after her
  return to the game she loves.

**RETURN OF A CHAMPION
THE MONICA SELES STORY**

RETURN OF A CHAMPION

THE
MONICA SELES STORY

JOE LAYDEN

St. Martin's Paperbacks

RETURN OF A CHAMPION: THE MONICA SELES STORY

Copyright © 1996 by Joe Layden

Cover photograph © Peter Gifford/Gamma Liaison.

ISBN: 0-312-96002-6

Printed in the United States of America

St. Martin's Paperbacks edition/July 1996

10 9 8 7 6 5 4 3 2 1

ACKNOWLEDGMENTS

Although there is only one name on this book, numerous people contributed to its publication. My thanks, first, to esteemed agent/packager Frank Coffey, who conceived the project, and to Tony Seidl, who sold it. At St. Martin's Press, special notice goes to editors Shawn Coyne and Todd Keithley. I am particularly grateful for the assistance of the Women's Tennis Association Communications Department, which provided a wealth of historical and statistical information. Thanks, also, to the writers who were kind enough to share thoughts and observations on the insular world of professional tennis, most notably Darrell Fry of the *St. Petersburg Times* and Wayne Coffey of the New York *Daily News*. And, as always, deepest thanks to my wife, Sue, who not only tolerated the madness this time, but also toiled as a research assistant—free of charge.

—Joe Layden

TABLE OF CONTENTS

RETURN OF A
CHAMPION

THE
MONICA
SELES
STORY

Prologue

WELCOME BACK

They call it Super Saturday.

On the penultimate day of the U.S. Open, six of the greatest athletes in the world join forces to stage an epic sporting event: seven, eight, maybe nine hours of tennis, enough to satisfy even the most ardent fan.

This late-summer festival from the National Tennis Center in Flushing Meadow, New York, includes two men's semifinals and a women's championship. Three potentially great matches, one after another. The concept generally has received good reviews over the years, particularly from advertisers who covet the sport's well-heeled audience. There is, however, an unfortunate flaw in the format. You see, the women are not really sharing the spotlight with the men on Super Saturday; they are standing in the shadows, supporting players in a male-dominated drama.

Most of the time, anyway.

September 9, 1995, was different—although it was a Saturday. And it was super. Beneath a bright New York sun, a crowd of 19,883 filed into Louis Armstrong Stadium, fully expecting the performers to hit all the high notes. They expected to see a mesmerizing confrontation between Jim Courier and Pete Sampras. They expected defending champion and number-one seed Andre Agassi to be at his best against Boris Becker.

As tantalizing as those matchups were, though, they were not the main attraction. They were merely bookends. For in between the two men's semifinals was the match of the year ... the match of the decade. *The match of the century?*

Too strong, perhaps. But then, it was a day, and a tournament, that begged for a bit of hyperbole. Shortly after Sampras had vanquished Courier, the Stadium Court was cleared and the crowd fell silent. The air was thick with anticipation. *When would she arrive? How would she react?* Finally, the answers came. From the tunnel she emerged, the once and future champion. Louis Armstrong Stadium came to life, rumbling and rocking as she strolled into view. With her hair pulled back into a girlish ponytail and a black brace on her left knee, she reflected both the innocence of an earlier time and the pain of innocence lost.

On her face, though, there was nothing but joy. As the applause swelled, Monica Seles began to smile. She raised a hand and waved. This was what she had missed. Not just the thrill of competing. Not just the glorious shiver of a perfectly executed two-fisted backhand.

This.

The crowd. The noise. *The excitement.*

She had waited so long for this moment. She had come so far. It had been three years since her last appearance in New York. Monica had won the U.S. Open in 1992, just as she had won the French Open and Australian Open. She owned the game that year, ruled it as few players ever have. She came within a whisper of winning at Wimbledon, too, of becoming the youngest player to sweep the Grand Slam. Monica was only eighteen years old when she defeated Arantxa Sanchez Vicario that afternoon. She breezed to a second consecutive U.S. Open championship—her seventh Grand Slam title—and held the trophy aloft, for all the world to see. She was so proud, so happy.

So young.

Now she was older, wiser. In every sense of the word, she was . . . *stronger.* Life had done that to Monica. It had hurt her, tested her. On a tennis court in Hamburg, Germany, some twenty-eight months earlier, she had been brutally attacked by a sad and deluded man, a nobody who briefly became somebody through an act of violence. One moment Monica was safe, secure, happy. The next moment someone was invading her world, violating her, driving a knife into her back. Suddenly she was on the ground, bleeding through her shirt, crying, wailing, wondering: *Why?*

There were no answers then and there were no answers now. At least, none that made sense. For nearly two and a half years Monica drifted. She withdrew from the game she loved, and as a result, lost sight of who she was and what she was. She suffered mightily in that time. But on this perfect September afternoon, as she peeled off her warmup and felt the sun caress her skin, as she basked in the warmth of the applause, Monica knew. It was behind her now. Somehow, she had endured.

"It's amazing, the electricity you feel when you walk into this stadium," she would later say. "This is one of the reasons I came back—to feel the excitement again. And today, I definitely felt it."

Of course, the salute was not for Monica alone. It was also for her opponent, Steffi Graf, an exquisite player in her own right. They defined each other, really. Monica's prolonged absence had allowed Graf to seize control of the women's game, but no one knew better than Graf the hollow nature of that dominance. And no one knew better than Seles the burden that Graf had carried—a burden born of guilt and responsibility.

So there was more at stake here than trophies and prize money and computer rankings. For both Monica Seles and Steffi Graf, this match represented the final stage of the healing process. Everyone involved in the game of tennis expected that at some point the two champions would have their close encounter. They were young enough, and talented enough, to renew their rivalry, which had become one of the most compelling in sports. But virtually no one expected it to happen so soon.

Only a few months earlier Monica was still in exile. Physically, she had recovered; emotionally, though, she still ached. She had played just one tournament prior to the Open—in Toronto—and while she was admittedly dazzling in that event, it seemed unreasonable to expect her to win six consecutive matches in her first Grand Slam tournament in three years. She was, after all, only human.

Or so it seemed heading into the New York fortnight. But now, on this most splendid of Saturdays, the questions about Monica's fitness and fortitude began to fade; like the years, they melted away, revealing an athlete of incomparable skill and a young woman of uncommon courage.

As the crowd settled in, Monica unsheathed her racquet and walked to the end line. She began to warm up, bouncing gently, shifting her weight from side to side—one fluid stroke after another. In a moment, the match would begin. Nearly twenty thousand people had come to see her play tennis, but Monica betrayed not a hint of nervousness. In fact, she appeared almost tranquil. Her eyes were bright, full of life.

Win or lose, she knew, it was a fine day.

Chapter 1

TOM AND JERRY

Monica Seles was five and a half years old the first time she picked up a tennis racquet. She pulled on a headband—a bow to her idol, the great Swedish player Bjorn Borg—and strolled outside for practice session number one with her father.

It seemed, at first glance, a typical prologue to a typical tale. Every day, all over the world, parents introduce their children to the game of tennis. Some merely hope to pass on their affection for the sport. Others—the athletic equivalent of stage mothers—have something else in mind. They see greatness in those tiny limbs, or at least the potential for greatness. They see the child at the net volleying like Pete Sampras, or five feet behind the baseline blasting forehands like Andre Agassi. Blinded by love or avarice or ego, or some combination of the three, they look at their progeny and think they see a prodigy. They see fame and fortune. They see dollar signs.

And so they buy the best clothes and the best shoes and the best equipment, they hire the best instructors, and pretty soon the kid's life revolves around tennis. Day and night. Whether he likes it or not. It doesn't last, though. Eventually he discovers that he lacks the talent or the drive . . . or whatever . . . to succeed as a professional. His parents are disappointed. He is demoralized. But life goes on. If he's lucky, the scars do not run deep. He adjusts, adapts, and harbors no resentment toward Mom and Dad, who must bear the responsibility for a childhood lost.

That, sadly, is a tennis story.

It is not, however, the Monica Seles story. Not even close.

She was born on December 2, 1973, in Novi Sad, Yugoslavia, the second and last child of Karolj and Esther Seles. Her mother was a computer programmer, her father an award-winning illustrator, documentary filmmaker, and physical education teacher. They made their home in a village near the Hungarian border; in fact, Hungarian was the language spoken in the Seles household.

Karolj was a gentle, philosophical man who happened to love athletics, so it was natural that he encouraged both Monica and her older brother, Zoltan, to participate in sports. Karolj, in his youth, had been a track and field star—

one of the top triple jumpers in Europe. He believed that through sports a child could find strength of character. He believed, as the ancient Greeks did, that a person was obligated to develop the body as well as the mind. But he also believed that life was too short and too precious to toil long and hard at something unpleasant. He understood intuitively what so many coaches either ignore or forget: the importance of having *fun*.

Two weeks after presenting his daughter with her first tennis racquet, Karolj listened intently and patiently as she gave a "retirement" speech. Already, she'd had enough. Forget about Borg— there were other role models for a little girl. In time, she'd find one.

Karolj wasn't the least bit angry with Monica. It wasn't his way to be hurt or upset. It was his way to move on. As a teenager during World War II he had been introduced to the ugly side of life. He had witnessed events that saddened and shadowed him, that threatened to make him a prisoner of his own memory. But Karolj would have none of that. He had seen his father devastated by the lingering effects of cruelty and savagery, and the lesson he learned was this: Sometimes you have to let go; you have to forget.

Jakab Seles was a deeply religious man who had taken a stand during World War I. In the heat of battle, he had refused to fire his gun; he would not kill another human being. Outraged by his passivity, a group of soldiers blindfolded

Jakab and dumped him in a foxhole, along with a gun. As he stood there, shaking with fright, they began firing shots into the air around him. The men figured if Jakab feared for his life, he would at least try to defend himself. They were wrong.

"My father did not pick up the gun," Karolj Seles told *Sports Illustrated* in a 1995 interview. "But for many years after that the terror stayed with him in his head."

Like his father, Karolj did not condone violence. But he did believe in fighting. Or, at least, in fighting back. Tyranny was not to be tolerated. In 1980 when the United States led a boycott of the Summer Olympics in Moscow, Karolj published a provocative cartoon in which the five Olympic rings were depicted as the barrels of a tank—emblematic of the Soviet Union's occupation of Afghanistan. "Russia like, no," Karolj told a *Sports Illustrated* reporter in 1991, in his own peculiar, yet endearing brand of fractured English. "This one get trouble, me."

Whatever ambition Karolj may have had for his little girl, he set it aside when she declared her lack of interest. Someday, perhaps, she would change her mind, and when that happened, he would welcome her back with open arms and a broad smile. And they would start anew. Until then, he would continue to work with Zoltan, who had become a pretty respectable player in his own right.

Two years later, Karolj was rewarded for his

patience. Appropriately enough, though, the revelatory moment that brought eight-year-old Monica back to the tennis court had nothing to do with a passion for the game; rather, like any child, she watched the trophies piling up in her brother's room and felt a rush of envy. When Zoltan won a national junior title in 1982, the excitement surrounding his accomplishment triggered a response in Monica: She, too, wanted to be an athlete. "All his friends would come home to admire [his trophies]," Monica recalled during a 1992 interview with *Vogue* magazine. "And I thought, 'This could be fun!' "

With Karolj serving as her mentor, there was virtually no chance that it *wouldn't* be fun. He had not been a player himself, but somehow he had turned that fundamental flaw into a strength. He pored over instructional manuals, he watched viedotapes, he learned as much as he could about the game. And then he went to work. It helped, obviously, that Karolj understood the athlete's needs. He had, after all, been a world-class performer in track and field, and he had not reached that level of achievement without acquiring a certain degree of insight into training—both physiological and psychological.

When dealing with an eight-year-old, however, the emphasis was not on technique or conditioning or developing mental toughness. The emphasis was on enjoyment. As he had with Zoltan, Karolj started slowly with Monica. Instead of taking her to a public or private tennis court, where she might be intimidated by the surroundings, he took her to the parking lot outside their apartment building. There, Karolj would hang a strand of rope between the bumpers of two cars and urge Monica to hit the ball over the "net."

A truly innovative teacher, Karolj never lost sight of the fact that Monica was just a child. Even as she developed and graduated to practice sessions on real tennis courts, he would not allow their workouts to feel like work. To encourage and amuse Monica, he sometimes drew pictures of her favorite cartoon characters—Tom and Jerry—on the tennis balls. If she came upon a ball with Tom's picture on it, she would pretend she was Jerry and smack it with all her might. Occasionally, Karolj would even place a toy stuffed animal on the court. Then he would ask Monica to try to hit the animal with a tennis ball. If she was successful, he gave her the toy.

Actually, Monica would later tell *People* magazine, "Even if I didn't hit it, I'd get it. But it made me want it even more."

Karolj was a master at the subtle art of motivation. He never screamed or insulted his pupil. If he manipulated, he did so in a way that was meant to enlighten and instruct. While it has been embraced by countless coaches throughout history, humiliation was not then, and is not now, part of Karolj Seles's educational repertoire. His relationship with Monica was built on mutual respect.

During an interview with *World Tennis* magazine early in her professional career, Monica told noted sports psychologist and author Dr. Jim Loehr, "I'm very close to my father. We're as close as a father and daughter could be. Our personalities are almost the same. He's never been tough with me. I've never had problems with my father on the court. He's very gentle, and I respect what he says about tennis and training."

Loehr supported that contention after observing the Seleses at work. "Monica's relationship with her father is unique," Loehr wrote. "I've never seen either one get upset with the other on court. The atmosphere is always one of great sensitivity and warmth."

Karolj's unorthodox teaching methods produced a highly unorthodox player. Monica, a natural lefty, was encouraged to swing with two fists on both sides of the ball. So, while her backhand was natural—with the right hand on top—her forehand was awkward. In order to execute it properly, Monica had to run around the ball and twist her body into the shot. This type of grip placed serious demands on its user: It required greater concentration and speed than a traditional forehand; moreover, it reduced the player's reach. For that reason, virtually no one—certainly no respected teaching professional—recommended its use.

Karolj Seles did, though. Where others saw weakness, he saw strength.

"My father wanted her to play that way, and

she accepted it," Zoltan told *Sports Illustrated.*
"She likes it that way."

Almost from the very beginning, the two-
fisted forehand was one of Monica's greatest
weapons. She was a tiny yet tireless girl, capable
of running down every ball, chasing it into the
corner, contorting her body like a corkscrew, and
then—*whap!*—ripping a winner down the line.
With each powerful stroke, Karolj would smile.

Unorthodox? Perhaps. Effective? Absolutely.

But was the coach a genius . . . or merely
lucky?

"My father transferred his professional knowledge from movies and cartoons to Monica's
game," Zoltan told *World Tennis.* "His cartoon
work helped him notice mistakes in movement
and technique. His drawings also helped Monica
to better understand the corrections."

Zoltan's opinion was echoed by Monica. "My
father's animated cartoons really helped me
learn the right service motion," she said. "And
because he used cartoons and lots of humor, I
always enjoyed practicing."

Within a few months Karolj realized his
daughter was not just another moderately talented kid who had benefitted from an early start.
She was . . . unique. She could practice for hours
on end, never complaining, never whining,
never losing focus. She absorbed everything, like
a sponge. And she seemed to actually *enjoy* the
workouts.

Karolj could only marvel at Monica's speed

and power. Where did it come from? She did not look like an exceptional athlete then, anymore than she does today. But she was blessed in less obvious ways: She had huge hands, with long, delicate fingers—artist's hands—and, like some Pinball Wizard of the tennis scene, *such a supple wrist*.

That elasticity produced a slingshot effect each time she swatted the ball, prompting more than one observer to stand slack-jawed at the sight of the eight-year-old with the professional ground-stroke, a little waif of a girl capable of throttling opponents ten years her senior. Looking back, even Monica herself had trouble comprehending her rapid development.

"I've seen the tapes, and I really can't believe it," she told *Vogue*. "It's unbelievable how hard I could hit the ball at that age."

Monica was only nine years old when she won the Yugoslavian twelve-and-under championship, a feat made even more impressive by the fact that she barely understood the parameters of the sport. To her, it was simple: Hit the ball, run, hit the ball again. Beyond that, well, Monica knew nothing. She did not even know how to keep score—she kept turning to Zoltan, a constant companion during tournaments, and asking whether she was winning or losing.

Usually, of course, she was winning. If Monica had only a rudimentary understanding of the rules of the game, she knew enough to keep moving, to keep swinging. Most important of all, she had talent her opponents could only imagine.

In 1984, at the age of ten, Monica won the European twelve-and-under championship. In 1985, as an eleven-year-old, she not only defended her European title, but was named Yugoslavia's Sportswoman of the Year—a remarkable accomplishment considering no one under the age of eighteen had ever before won the award.

It was also in 1985 that Monica finished first in the twelve-and-under division of the Orange Bowl tournament in Miami. There she caught the attention of instructor Nick Bollettieri, whose respected tennis academy in Bradenton, Florida, included such future stars as Andre Agassi and Jim Courier. Bollettieri sat in the stands beneath the glowing south Florida sun, working on his infamous tan, when he was suddenly riveted by what he saw: a scrawny kid, all arms and legs, scrambling around the court like a waterbug, pausing only to take the ball on the rise and smack it back at her opponent with such ferocity that it took his breath away.

Bollettieri had seen a lot in his day. He had worked with some of the best players in the game. But this player, this ... *child* ... was different. He knew right away: She was the type of athlete who came along once in a lifetime. She was special. She was *brilliant*.

"I was so impressed that I offered Monica a full scholarship and invited the entire family to

come and live at the academy," Bollettieri told
World Tennis. "She was all feet and could barely
see over the net. But could she play!"

The Seleses were an extremely close-knit family, supportive and loving, but wary of outsiders.
Still, Karolj understood what the offer meant.
And so did Monica. She was not even a teenager,
but she knew what she wanted: to become one
of the best tennis players in the world. For a
number of reasons, that goal would likely prove
elusive if she remained in Novi Sad. In his 1993
book, *Ladies of the Court: Grace and Disgrace on the
Women's Tennis Tour,* author Michael Mewshaw
discussed with Seles the factors that contributed
to her decision to pull up roots at such a tender
age.

"In my town there wasn't even an indoor
court," Monica noted. "And you can't be a top-
ten player if you can't play for five or six months
in winter. Only football and basketball seem to
count in Yugoslavia. It was hard to fight to get
a court, to fight for everything."

Additionally, Seles said, there were more opportunities in the United States for girls who
wanted to participate in athletics. In Yugoslavia,
she faced a double dose of discrimination: the
first as a tennis player, the second as a female.

"There's the whole attitude toward girls," she
said. "Everybody thought I was crazy and my
parents were crazy when I wanted to be an athlete, and there were all these discussions about
whether it was good for me to play tennis. I

think it's not good for a child to have to listen to all this. That's why I had to leave."

So in 1986, at the age of twelve, Monica packed her bags. Accompanied at first only by Zoltan, who had just received his discharge from the army, she set out for America: land of milk and honey . . . and year-round tennis.

Chapter 2

COMING TO AMERICA

When Monica arrived in 1986, the Nick Bollettieri Tennis Academy had approximately 180 students, all between the ages of eleven and eighteen. Another twenty pupils sat on a waiting list, eager to shell out twenty thousand dollars annually for the privilege of attending the most famous—and demanding—tennis school in the world.

Bollettieri himself was an intriguing, complex man who had risen from humble roots in North Pelham, New York, to a place of prominence in the glitzy world of professional tennis. That he was one of the most knowledgeable and effective instructors in the game could not be denied, and yet, Bollettieri had more than his share of critics, in part because he lacked the proper pedigree as a player.

In fact, Bollettieri did not begin playing tennis until he was eighteen years old. He quickly fell in love with the game, though, and started coaching when he was in the U.S. Army. He attended law school at the University of Miami, but failed to obtain a degree. After dropping out, he began giving tennis lessons in North Miami Beach for the princely sum of $1.50 per hour.

By '86, of course, the fee had risen substantially. Bollettieri was a teaching and promotional wizard who first gained widespread notoriety as the cofounder of the Port Washington Tennis Academy in New York. In 1978, armed only with big ideas and an ability to work eighteen hours a day for months on end, Bollettieri left Port Washington and opened his twenty-two-acre academy in Bradenton. He started with a mere twenty-five students, but it wasn't long before word of the academy spread. Soon, he no longer needed to recruit pupils: They came to him. So, too, did the sponsors: Nike, Subaru, and Prince, among others.

Their support allowed Bollettieri not only to earn a very nice living, but also to expand and improve the facilities and services offered. By the time Monica Seles showed up, the Nick Bollettieri Tennis Academy was generally considered the best in the business. Already it had provided a springboard to stardom for players such as Jimmy Arias, Aaron Krickstein, Carling Bassett, and Paul Annacone. Agassi and Courier—in their midteens at the time—were soon to follow.

Of course, there was a price to pay for attending the Bollettieri Tennis Academy, a fee not covered by the initial twenty grand. Students generally were plucked from home and hearth and deposited in a strange and serious land. Typically, they had no idea what they were getting into until they arrived. When the awakening came, it was often a shock. They felt they had enrolled in summer camp, when in fact they had enlisted in Bollettieri's Army.

The drill instructor was a fifty-five-year-old ex-paratrooper who believed in order . . . and in discipline. He and his staff of sixty-five instructors expected students, regardless of their age, to work as hard as they could. Bollettieri lived that way. He pushed himself relentlessly, and while the cost was admittedly steep (he had been married five times), so were the rewards. His students were compelled to recognize this simple equation: Without sacrifice, there is no chance for success. To that end, the academy was run like a boot camp. Students attended one of two local private schools during the morning, then trained feverishly in the afternoon. At night, they studied. They were not allowed to watch TV or call their parents during the week. Lights were turned off promptly at 10:30 P.M.

It was a demanding routine, but one Bollettieri vigorously defended. "I'd like to know how to run a place with all these kids without discipline," he told *People* magazine in 1986. "I like a neat, orderly place. That's why I loved the paratroopers. And that's what I want here."

Not everyone thrived on Bollettieri's highly regimented diet. For some students, the pain and isolation proved unbearable. "I'd say we have about three or four casualties during the school year," Bollettieri said. "This kind of life is a shock. They're not prepared for it. Maybe they're too young, maybe they miss their mommy and daddy."

Today, Bollettieri's academy has evolved into a more humane place. Perhaps because he has mellowed with age, there is less yelling, less pressure. He has adopted a more patient, holistic approach in which students are encouraged to develop as human beings as well as athletes before embarking on professional careers. "Too many of our kids didn't have complete enough games when they went out on the tour," Bollettieri told *Tennis* magazine's Peter Bodo in September 1995. "And their tennis education was so intensive that they didn't have the other mental and emotional tools they needed to deal with the stress and grind of the tour, not to mention normal life. A lot of the criticisms leveled against us were justified, but we were working on a frontier."

Into that brave new world walked Monica Seles. Unlike the great majority of her fellow students, Monica did not live in a dorm room. Instead, she and Zoltan shared a two-bedroom condo near the academy. Though he was only twenty-one years old and quite an accomplished player in his own right, Zoltan had temporarily abandoned any career plans so that he could help Monica. Karolj and Esther had agreed that Monica should accept Bollettieri's scholarship offer, but they did not want her living alone. The plan was for Zoltan to serve as a surrogate father for his twelve-year-old sister for a few months. Then, if all was going well—if Monica was enjoying and benefitting from her experience—Esther and Karolj would join their children in the United States.

Inevitably, Monica suffered from culture shock and homesickness during those early days. But, as Bollettieri would soon discover, she was an extremely tough and resilient child. Despite the emotional upheaval in her life, Monica was able to focus exclusively on the task at hand. Already fluent in French, Hungarian, and Serbo-Croatian, she quickly mastered English and became an exceptional student at Bradenton Academy. On the tennis court, while others wilted beneath the heat of the Florida sun, exhausted by Bollettieri's conditioning drills, Monica kept chugging along.

She was so small, and yet so strong. Jim Loehr, who has followed Monica's career since she arrived in the U.S., wrote in *Tennis World*, "From the first day I saw Seles hit the ball, I could see she was different, *very* different. For starters, she can practice for hours at a time and never lose concentration, get upset, or utter a negative word. Pound for pound, she hits the ball harder than anyone I've ever seen."

Darrell Fry, tennis writer for the *St. Petersburg*

Times, had a similar reaction. "I remember the first time I saw Monica the thing that really struck me was her concentration," Fry recalled. "I had never seen anything like it. She was just a little kid, but she was so focused. Nothing bothered her."

For a while Monica remained Bollettieri's secret weapon, a mystery even to many of her fellow students. It wasn't long, though, before word got out. Eventually, the other girls at the academy refused to practice with her. Understandable, really. They took no pleasure in serving as cannon fodder for a pip-squeak like Monica. So, Bollettieri was forced to turn to some of his older male students. That didn't work for long, either.

"Nick ordered me to hit with Monica one day," Jim Courier told *Sports Illustrated.* "First ball, *whap!,* she smacks a winner. Next, *whap!,* winner. I said, 'O.K., I'm impressed. You can play. Now let's practice.' Uh-uh. *Whap, whap, whap.* After fifteen minutes I walked off. I told Nick, never again. He could get another guinea pig."

Occasionally Bollettieri enlisted the services of established players on the women's professional tour to serve as hitting partners for his protege, but they, too, found the experience most unpleasant. Monica was only twelve years old, but her relentless march toward greatness was now in full stride.

*   *   *

Six months after Monica left the nest, Karolj and Esther flew after her. Esther had secured a two-year leave of absence from her job, and Karolj had decided to put his career on hold. The entire family moved into a small apartment in Bradenton and began building a proper network of support for their budding superstar. Zoltan worked with Monica on conditioning, Bollettieri on technical skills. As he had been from the beginning, Karolj was involved in all aspects of her training—although a few years down the road, when Monica split with Bollettieri, Karolj's precise role would be a source of contention. For now, though, they all got along famously.

"Equally impressive is the dedication of the Seles family," Bollettieri wrote in a column for *World Tennis* in 1987. "They have one goal—to make Monica number one in the world. Every move is calculated toward achieving this objective. . . . Zoltan spends between five and eight hours per day on the court with Monica. Their offcourt training routine is also something to behold: Footwork, quickness drills, dodging, diving, jumping, throwing, catching, running forward, backward, and sideways are all daily activities. I have never seen such total dedication in an athlete."

During her first two years at the Bollettieri Tennis Academy, Monica did not play any matches. Bollettieri and Karolj agreed that even though she was quite capable of playing against professionals—and, of course, destroying other juniors—

there was no need to rush Monica. Surprisingly enough, considering her natural tendency to fight, and to compete, Monica embraced this approach. "Taking the pressure off helped me develop more," she told *World Tennis* in 1989. "I could work on all kinds of new things and never worry about winning or losing."

In Bollettieri's laboratory, the subject of this experiment flourished. Visitors treated to a glimpse of one of Monica's practice sessions were often stunned to the point of speechlessness. They would watch this five-foot-two, ninety-pound child rushing madly about the court, throttling one ball after another, each shot accompanied by a guttural cry that seemed to rise from her very soul. . . .

"Unnnhhhh-EEE!"

And they could not believe what they were seeing.

Monica was not yet into self-promotion, and Karolj and Esther barely spoke English. So, it was Bollettieri's job to describe this remarkable work-in-progress.

"It's hard to single out the one or two most impressive qualities about Seles," he wrote in *World Tennis* in '87. "Her timing is incredible: She has the ability to stand inside the baseline and pick up everything on the rise. This quality also gives her surprising power for her size. Monica rarely hits a ball down the center, opting instead to move her opponents from side to side while they are pinned to the baseline. But don't think that she is only a baseliner. She is a relentless attacker, always looking for the opportunity to come to the net and end the point. . . .

"There are no guarantees in the world of tennis," Bollettieri said by way of conclusion. "No one is a sure bet. But I would wager that within the next three to five years a lot of knowledgeable tennis people may be echoing my assessment."

Sooner than that, as it turned out. Monica played in her first professional tournament, the Virginia Slims of Florida, in March 1988. She had grown to five-foot-five and one hundred pounds by then, but still hardly cut an imposing figure on the tennis court. Looks do not always tell the entire story, though, as Helen Kelesi discovered. Kelesi, ranked number thirty-one in the world at the time, took the court at the Polo Club of Boca Raton fully expecting to advance easily into the second round. Word of Monica's talent had drifted east from Bradenton, but the fact remained: She was an unranked, fourteen-year-old amateur playing in a professional tournament. If not for the kindness of tournament director George Liddy, who gave her a wildcard entry, Monica would have been forced to endure several days of qualifying matches. It was only reasonable to presume that against eighteen-year-old Helen Kelesi, she was in over her head.

Within the first two minutes of their match, however, it was apparent that Monica was right

where she belonged. Not only did she not lose
the match to Kelesi, she did not even lose a set.
Monica advanced with a stunning 7–6 (7–3), 6–3
victory. Not surprisingly, after putting up a respectable fight in losing to Chris Evert, 6–2, 6–1,
in the second round, Monica became something
of a curiosity. Suddenly reporters wanted to talk
to her. Sponsors wanted to meet with her.
Agents were swarming.

Monica found it all to be a bit dizzying. During the Virginia Slims of Florida she was so shy
and soft-spoken that she declined to answer reporters' questions from a podium; rather, she
pulled up a chair and asked the media to gather
round. Through a mouthful of braces, in hushed
tones, she tried to discuss her goals. "I don't
want to hurry myself," she said. "But every person who plays tennis wants to be number one in
the world."

One week later, at the Lipton Championships
in Key Biscayne, Florida, the tennis community
was put on notice: Monica was no one-hit wonder. She was a player. She overwhelmed 140th-
ranked Louise Field, 6–0, 6–3, in the first round,
and then gave seventeen-year-old Gabriela Sabatini—by then a top-five player—all she could
handle before losing, 7–6, 6–3.

And then, as quickly and suddenly as she had
emerged, Monica disappeared. She returned to
Bradenton. Back to school, back to practice, back
to her family. For the rest of the year, there
would be no more professional tournaments.

"Her father and brother contend that there's no reason to rush her," Bollettieri explained to the *Miami Herald*. "We're more concerned with her technique and that there are no more injuries and that she's having fun and getting bigger and stronger."

Their strategy was sound. Nevertheless, it prompted bemusement in tennis circles because it was just so . . . unusual. Children with Monica's talent are not often protected in this way. Sadly, they are often exploited. They play too much, too soon. They burn bright and fast, and then fade away. Not Monica, though. She was no comet. She was a star.

Monica made her debut as a professional in February 1989 at the Virginia Slims of Washington. She reached the semifinals, defeating, in succession, Larisa Savchenko, Robin White, and Manuela Maleeva-Fragniere. Along the way she did not lose a set. In her semifinal match against Zina Garrison, however, a nagging ankle injury forced Monica to default. She was, of course, disappointed. But she also knew there would be other tournaments, other opportunities.

Three months later, at the Virginia Slims of Houston, fifteen-year-old Monica collected her first winner's check. After proclaiming that she had only "a five percent chance to win," Monica upset Chris Evert, 3–6, 6–1, 6–4. Afterward, Evert seemed to be one of the few people in the building not stunned by the outcome. "If you lose to someone who's not a good player, then you should be concerned," Evert said. "But Monica's a good player."

By the time June rolled around, as Monica was preparing for her first Grand Slam tournament, there was no longer any chance that she would surprise an opponent. The word was out: Monica Seles was, in all likelihood, the game's next great player. As Jim Loehr wrote in *World Tennis* just before the French Open, "Her variety of spins, angles, and pace is mind-boggling. Seles pounds the ball from inside the baseline, hits it on the rise, and punishes short balls. She grunts like Jimmy Connors and breathes the same fiery intensity."

As she became more comfortable in the spotlight, she also displayed a theatrical flair rarely seen in the sedate world of women's tennis. At the French Open, for example, Monica defeated a pair of Americans, Ronni Reis and Stacey Martin, in the first two rounds. Then, in her first appearance on Court Central, the game's newest sensation made a sensational entrance, giggling and waving, tossing flowers into the stands. Before the match began, however, she nearly crossed the line separating showmanship from bad taste when she offered a bouquet to her opponent, Zina Garrison, who was not even slightly amused.

"It's a bunch of hype," an obviously irritated Garrison said after losing the match, 6–3, 6–2. "She's just another baseliner."

No, she wasn't. By the time Stade Roland Garros fell silent, Monica had established herself as the player most likely to challenge Steffi Graf's stranglehold on the number-one ranking. She lost to Graf, 6–3, 3–6, 6–3, in a gripping semifinal that left the tennis aficionado salivating at the prospect of a long and healthy rivalry.

And if the tournament was something of a disappointment for Graf, who lost in the final to clay-court specialist Arantxa Sanchez Vicario, it was an unqualified success for Monica. "I had nothing to lose," she said after her match with Graf. "She's been beating everyone, 6–0, 6–1, so I am just hoping to get one game off her. I didn't expect anything here. Grand Slam. Two weeks. On clay. I'm happy. It doesn't matter I lost. I'm going to lose to worse players than her."

Not often, though. Monica played well at both Wimbledon and the U.S. Open, reaching the fourth round of each tournament. Not surprisingly, she was named Rookie of the Year. As 1989 came to a close, Monica Seles—the "Baltic Basher," as one magazine had referred to her—was the sixth-ranked player in the world.

And climbing.

Chapter 3

SWEET SIXTEEN

Despite her meteoric rise through the computer rankings in 1989, Monica remained in the shadows as a new year dawned. Not that she wanted it that way, of course—she was, at sixteen years of age, hungry for publicity and more than a little naive about the media. Before becoming one of the most reclusive players in professional tennis, Monica was one of the most accessible. She chatted with reporters until their pens ran dry. She signed autographs until her hands cramped up. She fairly basked in the spotlight. Unlike some players on the women's tour, Seles actually seemed to crave the attention. To her, it was less an annoyance than a diversion, something to break the routine of endless hours of practice and matches and travel. The adoration was a fringe benefit, not a burden.

In the winter of 1990, though, Monica had yet to take her place in the pantheon of the game's stars. True, she had ascended from eighty-sixth in the rankings to number six as 1989 came to a close. But few people knew much about her. Tennis is an insular world, and its fans are among the most zealous in sports. But it takes more than a top-ten ranking to transcend the boundaries of the game. The true superstars are capable of winning a Grand Slam Tournament on a Sunday and taking a power lunch on a Monday. They appear to be comfortable with their fame and celebrity, even if they really aren't.

Monica wanted all of that, and was poised to achieve it. She was charming, gregarious, ambitious, and quirky—in an endearing sort of way. If she was prone to laughing like Woody Woodpecker or speaking at a hundred miles per hour in a voice that mixed English, Hungarian and, like, you know, Valley Girl, in a bizarre dialect that was strictly her own, she was unfailingly friendly and polite. The critical backlash to Monica's unique style of self-promotion would not peak for another year. For the time being, she was given the benefit of the doubt by all but a handful of people, mostly other players. She was generally seen as a positive force in the game of tennis, a player whose natural grace and good humor had to help the image of a sport in which the stars were too often viewed as robots.

Of course, it helped that she was immensely talented. With each powerful stroke Monica seemed to be trying to rip the cover off the ball.

In 1988 and 1989 she had been a child with the groundstroke of a woman. Now she was a young woman with the groundstroke of a man. A very strong man. As the new year began she was five foot seven inches tall and weighed 115 pounds. She appeared almost delicate—until she flailed away with that strange, two-fisted groundstroke, sending rockets down the sideline and deep into corners. If necessary, she could drop the right hand and hit with her left, but more often than not she was quick enough to run around the ball and crush a two-fisted forehand.

"It's the way I first picked up the racket," she once explained to *Sports Illustrated*. "So I stay with it."

And why not? No one hit the ball harder than Seles. No one hit with greater accuracy. So what if her approach was unusual. It worked, and that was all that mattered.

"She's so dangerous because of the angles she creates," Tommy Thompson, a noted coach at Harry Hopman International Tennis, told the *St. Petersburg Times*. "I think a lot of players can't relate to that. She can take the girls right off the court from the center of the court. She bangs, but she can open up the angles and still bang. You've got problems when you've got a girl who can do that."

Unlike her opponents, Monica had few problems. She was fortunate to have grown up in a family that truly seemed to have her best interests in mind. Once they moved to the United

States, Monica was the breadwinner. But she seemed to handle that pressure with relative ease. It helped that her parents were at once supportive and protective. Together they decided that Monica needed time off at the end of 1989. She had reached the quarterfinals in eight of her ten tournaments in '89, and clearly was in a position to make a run at the top five in the world. But she was, after all, just an adolescent. She was tired, even if she wasn't willing to admit it.

So, even as her star was rising, Monica retreated to the sidelines. For nearly two months she did not play a tournament. She even skipped the 1990 Australian Open. Such an approach flew in the face of conventional wisdom, but then, there was nothing conventional about Monica Seles or her family.

While this was happening, of course, Monica was presumably losing ground to other young tennis stars, most notably Jennifer Capriati. At only thirteen years of age, Capriati was a sensational talent with an equally appealing personality. Those prone to making such comparisons predicted a long and compelling rivalry between Seles and Capriati. But in early 1990, despite her lofty ranking and status as WTA Rookie of the Year, Seles was not nearly as famous, or wealthy, as her younger American counterpart. Capriati had signed numerous lucrative endorsement deals before she even made her professional debut. As Monica noted during an interview with the *St. Petersburg Times*, "In Yugoslavia, everyone knows me. But in America, it's a lot different."

It would not be different for long. With batteries recharged, Monica rejoined the tour in February 1990. Predictably, she struggled a bit and was upset in her first two tournaments. No one in her inner circle was ready to panic, though. Not Nick Bollettieri, not Monica's parents or brother, and certainly not Monica. She was having too much fun. They all realized that it would take her a few weeks, maybe even months, to regain her competitive edge. When that happened, Monica would resume her ascent through the computer rankings.

The first indication of Seles's potential for greatness—her "breakthrough" tournament—came in March, at the Lipton International Players Championships in Key Biscayne, Florida. Lipton was a substantial tournament, and Seles, who came into the event with a 3–3 record, was not expected to be much of a factor. Her play had been erratic, her confidence supposedly shaken. In truth, however, she was merely following a predictable path. She was a young, gifted athlete grunting and smashing her way toward greatness. At any moment, she was capable of breaking out of her slump—if it could even be called that—and decimating an entire field. That is what happened in Key Biscayne.

Seles rolled through the tournament, eventually defeating Judith Weisner in straight sets for her second tour victory.

If that triumph came as a surprise to some observers, it was not terribly shocking to Seles. She had, in fact, prepared for the possibility. In her first two years on the tour, Monica had played motivational games with herself. She would treat herself to a present each time she advanced through a round. "Usually, when I come to a tournament, I give bonuses to myself," she explained. "If I have a tough first-round opponent, then I usually pick out something that I like. And if I win, then I get it."

Monica had her eye on a new leather jacket, but for some reason decided to strike a new deal with herself at the Lipton International. This time, she would not run off to the store after a first-round victory. This time she would wait until the final day—until she had collected the $112,500 winner's check and the Waterford crystal trophy—before buying herself a gift.

Seles's road to the Lipton final was comparatively smooth—upsets to Capriati, Gabriela Sabatini, and Zina Garrison left her with only one opponent who was seeded in the top ten—but her performance was nonetheless impressive. In the final, she was overwhelming. Seles did not lose a serve and broke Weisner twice in each set for a quick, lopsided victory.

Weisner, ranked twenty-eighth, was playing in her first tournament final. The twenty-four-year-old Austrian did not fall victim to nerves, however; she simply couldn't deal with Seles's power from the baseline. For the first time in the new year, Monica's game was consistently sharp. She hammered away at Weisner, running her older, more experienced opponent all over the court. To complicate matters, just when Weisner thought she had Seles figured out, Seles would change the pace dramatically by flicking a neat drop shot over the net. Weisner, of course, had no chance.

"She's very clever," Weisner said. "I really had problems with her game. I couldn't guess where she was going to play. I was always a little bit late with my strokes.

"Her game is completely different than anybody else. I mean, I played against all the players, and it's really hard to get used to it. I just didn't find my rhythm."

Intentionally or not, Monica managed to disrupt her opponents' concentration in a number of ways. Her tennis game was so thoroughly unorthodox, so incongruously powerful for one so delicate, that the mere sight of her pounding winners was disconcerting. But that was only part of it. There was, too, the matter of Monica's tendency to grunt with each swing of the racket.

There is nothing unusual about an athlete using his or her voice to accompany a show of force. It's common in just about every sport. Rarely, though, had there ever been anything quite like the bark of Monica Seles. With stun-

ning speed she would chase down a ball deep
in the corner, wind up for a wicked two-fisted
forehand, and then..."*Unnnhhhh-EEE!*" The
strange sound that accompanied each stroke was
almost inhuman. It was described by one observer as sounding like a sneeze being choked
off. Ted Tinling, the legendary tennis historian—
who, before passing away in 1990 became quite
a fan of Monica's—said that when Seles hit the
ball, "she sounds like she's wringing the neck of
a Christmas goose."

Actually, Seles's grunting was nothing more
than a tool designed to give her more power. By
exhaling with great force, she was able to prepare her body and mind for the extreme stress
of hitting a tennis ball as hard as she could. It all
happened in a split second, with no thought
whatsoever, but it was a crucial aspect of Monica's game, as natural to her as breathing.

Unfortunately, not everyone saw it—or heard
it—that way. Seles's grunting escalated in volume with each shot, which made long rallies almost painful for fans and players alike.
Tolerance was the rule when she was a rookie,
struggling to find her place in the grown-up
world of tennis. But now, as it became apparent
that she was one of the best players in the game,
regardless of her age, annoyance seemed to be
the most common reaction. In April, during the
U.S. Hard Courts Championship in San Antonio,
Texas, one player, Katerina Maleeva openly criticized Seles for her grunting. Annoyance had

now become anger. For her part, Monica was bewildered. "You know," she said, "I don't even know when I'm doing it."

The implication, of course, was that Monica couldn't possibly be held accountable for behavior she couldn't recognize; you couldn't very well ask her to turn down the volume when she wasn't even aware that she was making any noise. Grunting was a part of her game, just as it was a part of Jimmy Connors's game. Interestingly, for all of his boorish behavior, no one ever requested that Connors stop barking like a seal. More likely, they thought it was merely a sign of his "competitive" nature. In the case of Seles, there were overtones of sexism in the criticism. Somehow, by gritting her teeth and hitting the hell out of the ball—and by shouting at the top of her lungs when ball met racket—Monica was challenging traditional notions of femininity. So, not only did the noise irritate her opponents, it also made spectators and advertisers and tournament directors squirm.

Thankfully, not everyone felt compelled to make Monica's grunting such a major source of controversy. As Cindy Hahn wrote in *Tennis* magazine, "With the robotic demeanors of [Ivan] Lendl and [Steffi] Graf putting the entire tennis-viewing community to sleep, the sound of Seles beats the sound of silence any day."

The furor over Monica's grunting ebbed and flowed. There was talk for a while of banning excessive grunting, as the Florida Tennis Association attempted in the early 1980s, but it quickly died. Seles herself attempted to curtail the habit, to no avail. Eventually, as people came to accept the grunting for what it was—Seles's signature—the controversy faded away. That, however, would take some time.

In the second week of May, Monica the tennis player, as opposed to Monica the noisemaker, won the Italian Open with surprising ease. For all of her grunting and giggling, Seles, at her core, was a ferociously competitive tennis player, a young woman who aspired not merely to win matches but to win every single point. She was not the type of player who thought about tanking a game or a set in order to conserve energy. It simply wasn't in her nature to concede anything. Her tendency to act like a nervous schoolgirl notwithstanding, she was perhaps the most driven player in women's tennis.

That particular side of Seles began to come into focus in Rome, where she eviscerated one of the game's greatest players, Martina Navratilova, in the final. Navratilova was thirty-three years old at the time, and clearly in the twilight of her career. But, as her triumph at Wimbledon in a few months would demonstrate, she was hardly a doddering old maid. Navratilova, in fact, played some of the best clay-court tennis of her life at the Italian Open, no small feat considering she was primarily a fast-court player. In the semifinals, Seles cruised past Helen Kelesi, losing only three games. Then she sat back and watched Navratilova fight gamely against the younger Sabatini. In a dramatic, exhausting match that took nearly two hours, Navratilova emerged a 7–6, 7–5 winner.

Sixteen hours later Navratilova was back on the court. Her thighs ached, her lungs burned. On the other side of the net was a player half her age, bouncing on fresh legs, ready to pounce on every shot, ready to take every ball on the rise and drill it to some remote corner of the court. The match was predictably gruesome. Seles, at the top of her game, ran Navratilova ragged. Had this been a grass-court match against a fully rested Navratilova, the outcome might have been different. But circumstances, and Seles's burgeoning talent and confidence, combined to make the Italian Open final one of the most lopsided in history. Precisely fifty-three minutes after she walked onto the court, Monica Seles walked off with a 6–1, 6–1 victory in hand. Navratilova, stunned by the ease with which she had been vanquished, could only mutter, "I feel like I've been run over by a truck."

For Seles, the match was significant not merely because it boosted both her ranking and her bank account, but because it came against one of the legendary players in the game. Indeed, she had never beaten Navratilova before. Now, there was only one player in the top ten she had not beaten: Steffi Graf. And Graf's ticket was about to be punched.

They met one week later, in the final of the

German Open in West Berlin. Graf was the top-ranked player in the world at the time, having won sixty-six consecutive matches; it was the second-longest winning streak in the modern era of tennis, surpassed only by Navratilova's seventy-four-match streak in 1984.

On this afternoon, though, Graf saw the future of tennis staring her in the face. At just a few weeks shy of twenty years of age, Graf was the finest player in the game, but Seles proved in West Berlin that the crown would no longer rest easily on Graf's head. To tennis fans this was wonderful news, for Graf had appeared to be nearly invincible over the course of the previous year. Women's tennis desperately needed a compelling rivalry, and on this day, one was born.

Seles, perhaps a bit unnerved, lost the first two games of the match before breaking Graf twice to take a 4–2 lead. She went on to win the match in straight sets, 6–4, 6–3. Both players attempted to downplay the significance of the match, since it was, after all, nothing more than a prelude to the upcoming French Open. But Seles couldn't help but betray a bit of satisfaction. "I'm much more experienced now," she said. "I wasn't afraid of Graf as much as before."

Those were the words of a confident, mature champion. In the next breath, however, Monica revealed herself to be a sixteen-year-old kid, albeit one with a knack for making even potentially obnoxious comments seem ingratiating. At a post-match press conference, for example, Seles was asked what she would do with the hundred thousand dollars she had received for winning the German Open. She thought for a moment and smiled.

"Maybe after the French Open I'll buy a car," she said. "I'm the only one of the top players who doesn't have a car. My taste is a little exotic—I would like a Lamborghini, but I'll settle for a red BMW."

No one bothered to point out that she was barely old enough to drive. It just didn't seem like the right thing to say at the time. Besides, if Monica played as well in Paris as she had played in Berlin, she'd be able to buy a fleet of BMWs.

Seles, the number-two seed, emerged as the favorite in Paris, but she was not the biggest story. In fact, she wasn't even in the top two. Graf endured intense media scrutiny because of a lurid little story featuring her father and manager, Peter Graf. On the third day of the French Open, European tabloids announced to the world that Peter Graf had not only been carrying on an affair with a French model named Nicole Meissner, but had also fathered her child. Peter Graf acknowledged the affair, but denied being the father of the child. Meissner filed a paternity suit against Peter Graf, but later, under oath, withdrew her charges and dropped the suit.

Still, the incident was sordid enough to provoke a tabloid feeding frenzy, which caused Steffi considerable pain. At each press conference she was asked to field intensely personal ques-

tions about her father, and it was fairly obvious
that she was under extreme emotional duress. As
John Feinstein wrote in his 1991 book *Hard
Courts*, Steffi Graf was "as rich, as famous, and
as talented as anyone could ever hope to be. And
as miserable as anyone could be."

As the tournament progressed, the other big
story at Roland Garros became . . . Jennifer Capriati. The French Open was Capriati's first
Grand Slam tournament—just one year earlier
she had become the youngest player ever to win
the French Open *junior* title, and now here she
was, barely fourteen years old, shredding the
competition in the grown-up tournament. She
laughed and smiled and did a lot of shopping
and sightseeing, usually with a television crew
in tow. Her childish vacuousness—she once referred to Napoleon as "that little dead dude"—
was oddly endearing. She delighted the fans.
Never mind that her career would be shattered
less than four years later, a victim of severe burnout; for the time being, Capriati was the darling
of the tennis world. In only her fifth professional
tournament she had become the youngest player
ever to reach the semifinals of a Grand Slam
event.

But Capriati was no match for Monica Seles.
Within minutes after stepping onto Court Central, Capriati's omnipresent smile faded. She was
baffled by Seles's stinging groundstrokes and
quickly lost the confidence that had sustained
her for nearly two weeks. Fearing that she would

be passed, Capriati stopped approaching the net and tried to engage Seles in a baseline battle, which she had no prayer of winning. Capriati also suffered from the jitters: Three times she double-faulted on break point. She did manage to save five match points, but eventually crumbled under the weight of Seles's relentless baseline attack.

"It's difficult for me on match points," Seles said after the 6–2, 6–2 victory. "I choked on them a lot."

An odd choice of words, considering she lost a total of just four games to Capriati, but then, Seles was often unintentionally hyperbolic. In the French Final she renewed her rivalry with Graf, who had dispatched Jana Novotna, 6–1, 6–2, in the semis. Despite the turmoil in her personal life, Graf was playing solid tennis and appeared quite capable of preventing Seles from winning her first Grand Slam title.

Until they began playing.

Seles won the first three games of the match and held a 3–1 lead when rain forced a fifty-five-minute delay. Graf fought back, though, and eventually forced a tiebreaker. Seles fell behind, 5–0, in the tiebreaker, but showed remarkable poise and heart in fighting back to win the set by a score of 7–6 (8–6). Blowing the tiebreaker sapped Graf of her spirit, and Seles easily won the second set, 6–4.

"Monica wasn't afraid of the risky play," Graf said afterward. "She showed much courage.

She's not a nightmare yet. I hope she's not becoming one."

In truth, she was. The victory was worth
$293,000 to Seles. It also made her the youngest
champion of a Grand Slam tournament in more
than a century. Not since fifteen-year-old Lottie
Dod won Wimbledon in 1887 had tennis seen
such a youthful champion. And with youth came
enthusiasm. Boundless, unabashed enthusiasm.
When the match ended Monica walked to the
net, politely embraced Graf, and then jogged off
in search of her father. In the chaos, though,
Monica could not reach Karolj; she could only
see him. The father removed his tie, pressed it to
his lips, and sent it through the stands to his
beloved and triumphant daughter. Monica took
the tie, kissed it, smiled, and sent it back.

The victory was complete.

Ironically, in the wake of her French Open victory, Monica received some of the harshest criticism of her career. Pointed remarks came from
all directions, most notably from Chris Evert.
The barbs had nothing to do with Seles's flawless
performance at Roland Garros; rather, they
stemmed from her refusal to acknowledge the
input of Nick Bollettieri in her remarkable ascent
to the top of the tennis world. The Seles family
and Bollettieri had parted ways in March 1990,
just a few months before the French Open. The
split was hardly amicable. In Paris, Monica was
vague in explaining her reasons for leaving

Bollettieri, saying only that there were "a lot of smaller reasons that we don't want to talk about."

According to several published reports, the dispute centered around the amount of time Bollettieri was spending with some of his other students, particularly Andre Agassi. Whatever the reason, the Seleses announced in the spring that they would no longer be associated with Bollettieri. In the future, Monica said, she would be coached exclusively by her father. That, of course, was painful enough for Bollettieri; what he found really distressing, though, was Seles's contention that Karolj had been her coach all along. He had taught her the game as a child, she said—which was true—and he had remained her primary teacher throughout their time in the United States. Bollettieri's contribution, she told *Sports Illustrated*, was to "help me with things off the court."

Bollettieri was understandably upset. After all, he had brought the Seles family to the United States and helped them establish residency near the grounds of the Bollettieri Tennis Academy. He worked with Seles each day. He asked for no compensation. The family did not pay rent. Not surprisingly, his response to being fired was anger. He claimed the Seleses owed him tens of thousands of dollars in training and living expenses. Monica disagreed. Her presence at the academy was beneficial to Bollettieri, whether he was getting paid or not. In the eyes of the world, he was the wizard behind Monica Seles, and surely that wasn't bad for business.

"It's a both-sides situation," Monica said. "We put lots of money into the academy. It's fifty-fifty."

Bollettieri didn't see it that way. He wanted to be compensated for his work; more than that, though, he wanted recognition from Monica herself. In his eyes, her departure was an insult. He was deeply hurt, and he wanted her to know it.

"If I wasn't her coach, I don't know what I did for those thousands of hours," Bollettieri told *Sports Illustrated*. "Not only did we put the time in on the court, we supported the whole family. They dispute everything."

As for his commitment to Monica's career, Bollettieri claimed complete allegiance. The Capriati family had approached him the previous fall, he said; his rejection was swift. "It took me about two minutes to make that decision," he told *Sports Illustrated*. "And I told Mr. Seles about it right away. 'Thank you, thank you,' he said."

Monica's decision to leave Bollettieri was, by most accounts, the right one. He was, in fact, spending most of his time with Agassi. If she erred, it was in simply failing to at least acknowledge that he had played a significant role in her development. This was the first major public relations blunder of her career, but its effect was hardly lethal. Some occasional sniping on both sides notwithstanding, the incident was gener-

ally considered old—and dull—news by the end
of the year.

During the Wimbledon fortnight, Bollettieri,
still bitter but apparently on the mend, announced that he would not take legal action
against the Seles family, even though he was
quite confident of victory. According to Bollettieri, teacher and pupil had operated for several
years on a handshake agreement; that agreement, as far as Bollettieri was concerned, was as
binding as any written contract. In sum, he took
the high road.

"It's not a question of them owing us,"
Bollettieri said in a story published in the *Miami
Herald.* "We did it with the understanding that
if she makes it, we all do. No contract was set
up. Her parents said they would take care of me
and the academy."

If Monica botched her breakup with Bollettieri,
she proved herself to be genuinely adept at handling other difficult situations. Indeed, for one so
young, she could be remarkably thoughtful and
mature. The day before Wimbledon was to begin, for example, there was Monica, strolling into
St. James Church in London to take part in a
memorial service for Ted Tinling, who had
passed away a few weeks earlier. It was expected
that many of the world's best female players
would show up to pay tribute to Tinling, a stylish gentleman who had long supported the
women's game. Sadly, most of the top players—

even those who knew Tinling well—found some
excuse to stay away. Perhaps it was too sad an
occasion; perhaps it simply wasn't convenient.

But Monica was there. She had come to know
Tinling in the last year of his life, and she liked
him immensely. The feeling was mutual. Tinling
saw something in Seles that reminded him of the
sport's glamorous past. And Seles saw in Tinling
a kind and slightly eccentric old man who loved
the game of tennis. It seemed to her that there
was no more appropriate place to be on the eve
of Wimbledon than at a service honoring his
memory.

"Ted was a great and wonderful man," Mon-
ica told *Sports Illustrated.* "At the end, I felt like
I knew him all my life."

Seles entered Wimbledon as the number-three
seed and the hottest player in the game. She had
won six consecutive tournaments and thirty-six
consecutive matches. But the tennis season is
long and demanding, and no one—not even
Monica Seles—is capable of playing flawlessly
every week. In the wake of her run through the
French Open, it was easy to forget that Monica
was still only sixteen years old. As talented and
driven as she was, she had much to learn about
the game. And grass was definitely not her favorite surface. Wimbledon favored the serve-
and-volley player; a baseline banger like Monica
was at a disadvantage.

Her second Wimbledon came to an end in the
quarterfinals, in a dramatic three-set loss to Zina

Garrison. Garrison, the number-five seed, was not a particularly big fan of the young superstar. They had met once before, in the third round of the 1989 French Open, and Garrison was still smarting from both the on-court spanking she received and Seles's shameless prematch grandstanding. As far as Garrison was concerned, Seles was a one-dimensional player who had gotten lucky a few times; a triumph of style over substance.

At Wimbledon, Garrison had a score to settle, and she did it in impressive fashion. She played one of the smartest matches of her life, confusing Seles with a stunning array of drop shots, half-volleys, and baseline winners. Monica, whose success stemmed largely from the fact that she never played defensively, was reduced to playing back on her heels. For the first time in recent memory, she seemed to lack confidence.

Not that victory came easily for Garrison; it didn't. She dropped the first set by a score of 6–3, won the second set by the same score, and then captured the deciding set, 9–7. In a post-match interview, Garrison had nothing but kind words for Seles. It was interesting: A year earlier, with the sting of defeat still fresh in her mind, she refused to give Seles her due; now, in victory, she was willing to concede the obvious.

"Monica was hitting the ball so unbelievably," Garrison said. "[In the first set] I felt I had been hit by something . . . I don't even know what I had been hit by. Even when I got going she was tough. I hit some great forehands down the line, and she'd hit them even better back down the same line. She could be the number-one player in the world very soon."

Not, however, by the end of the year. The U.S. Open in Flushing Meadow was one of the more disappointing tournaments of 1990 for Monica. Despite being upset at Wimbledon, she was expected to at least reach the semifinals in New York. The surface was ideal for her type of game—not too slow, not too fast—and she seemed to be in good spirits and good health. One of the wonderful things about being a six-teen-year-old tennis player is that no single defeat is devastating. Not even at Wimbledon.

Winning at the U.S. Open, however, is tricky business. The media pressure is intense. The traffic is unbearable. The crowds can be rude. There aren't enough practice courts. And, of course, there is the matter of shopping in Manhattan, which was perhaps the biggest distraction of all to a teenaged millionaire.

Considering all of the annoyances one is obliged to confront at the Open, it seemed almost ludicrous that upon arriving in New York, Seles was hit almost immediately with questions about her grunting. Her on-court squealing had been a source of great amusement throughout the year (in particular, at Wimbledon), but at Flushing Meadow, where the roar of passing jets often drowned out the noise of twenty thousand screaming spectators, how much of a distraction could it possibly be? The answer, apparently, was "substantial." For the first time since the tournament had moved from Forest Hills in 1978, air traffic was restricted during the U.S. Open. If Louis Armstrong Stadium was not exactly tranquil, it was at least quieter. Unfortunately, that placed the spotlight back on Seles. While whipping Elena Pampoulova of Bulgaria, 6–0, 6–0, in the first round, Monica appeared to be making a concerted effort to bite her tongue. Afterward, the press wanted to know whether this signaled the beginning of the end of her grunting phase.

Typically, Monica seemed more amused than irritated by the line of questioning. "I don't think I was grunting as bad," she said. "It is true that it wasn't too tough a match; maybe that is why I didn't grunt. I am getting better at it.

"I don't want everyone to ask me about it in every interview," she added. "I'll always have it a little bit, but it won't be as loud as it was before."

Not true. The volume depended largely on the importance and difficulty of the match. As the stress increased, so did the decibel level. Certainly Monica was back to her usual noisy self in the third round, when she was shocked by a twenty-four-year-old Italian named Linda Ferrando. Ferrando had practiced with Seles several months earlier, and had filled a mental notebook with images of Monica's strengths and weaknesses. Someday, she figured, it might come in handy. On the last day of August, Ferrando's preparation paid off as she employed an aggressive serve-and-volley attack to upset Seles, 1–6, 6–1, 7–6 (6–3), for the biggest victory of her career.

Like just about everyone who witnessed the match, Ferrando was practically speechless afterward. Monica, though, talked enough for both players. "I wasn't my usual self today," she said. "I've had a lot of bad matches before, but I just pulled them out. Today, on the important points, I just got too nervous."

The upset served as an ideal launching point for a debate on the relative wisdom and coaching skills of Karolj Seles and Nick Bollettieri. First, there was the matter of equipment. Monica had signed a lucrative endorsement deal with Yonex after Wimbledon, and felt compelled to use the new racquet (she had previously used a Prince) at the Open, even though she was not yet accustomed to it. That probably was not a wise move. Second, when Monica revealed that not only did she not remember practicing against Ferrando, she hadn't even bothered to ask her father to scout any of Ferrando's matches, it opened the door for Bollettieri to take a shot at the new regime.

"I had suggested to Monica to always keep a diary of other players," Bollettieri told the *Miami Herald*. "So, when she played, she would know something about them. But her father's the coach. It's his job as coach to do that."

The sniping continued the next day, when Andre Agassi was asked by reporters to comment on the Bollettieri-Seles feud. Agassi, a loyal Bollettieri disciple, was quick to rush to his teacher's defense. "You'll never hear me say Nick didn't coach me like Seles turned around and said," Agassi promised. And indeed, he never has.

As for Monica, she was eager to put the Bollettieri incident behind her—permanently—and concentrate on playing tennis. By the time the season-ending Virginia Slims Championships rolled around in late November, she had basically achieved that goal.

Few people expected much excitement or drama in the final days of the Slims, not without Navratilova (who had recently undergone arthroscopic knee surgery) and Graf (a first-round loser). As it happened, though, the final between Seles and Sabatini was one of the most engrossing, enjoyable matches of the year.

The Virginia Slims, no slave to convention, was the only tournament that offered the possibility of a five-set final. And that is precisely what Seles and Sabatini provided. In a thrilling match that captivated Madison Square Garden for nearly four hours, Seles defeated Sabatini, 6–4, 5–7, 3–6, 6–4, 6–2. It was the first professional five-set match between two women since 1901, when Elizabeth Moore defeated Myrtle McAteer in the U.S. Nationals.

Moore played a remarkable 105 games of singles over the course of two days that year. She was a strong, competitive woman, and the endurance test left no scars on her. Marion Jones, however, had staggered through the last few games of the all-comers final against Moore; her condition, and the prospect of other women being forced to endure such long matches, so concerned the male-dominated United States Lawn Tennis Association that it opted to shorten the finals of all women's matches to best-of-three sets. The decision, while perhaps born of good intentions, angered many of the top female players, including Moore. She, like many others, was particularly miffed at the fact that the United States Lawn Tennis Association neglected to consult any women about the matter—not even the athletes who had been involved in the 1901 marathon.

As Moore said at the time, "Lawn tennis is a game not alone of skill but of endurance as well, and I fail to see why such a radical change should be made to satisfy a few players who do not take the time or do not have the inclination to get themselves in proper condition for playing."

Thankfully, both Seles and Sabatini were equipped to handle the rigors of a five-set match. Sabatini was one of the strongest players on the tour; Seles, who had sprouted to five foot nine, 125 pounds by the end of the year, was one of the most resilient. Neither her diet nor her training regimen was quite what it should have been, but she compensated with youth and talent.

In fact, the most distressing part of the week for Monica was a trip to Bloomingdale's department store in Manhattan, during which she lapsed into a shopaholic haze and became separated from her parents. Seles spent more than an hour and a half trying to find Esther and Karolj. "It's not like the Sarasota Mall," she jokingly told *Sports Illustrated*. "It's crazy. I kept going around and around. It was a very long day."

A long day. A long week. A long year. But a wildly productive one, as well. As Thanksgiving gave way to Christmas, and the old year gave way to the new, Monica Seles celebrated her seventeenth birthday by moving up a notch in the computer rankings. She was the number-two player in the world. She had won nine tournaments and $1.63 million in 1990.

As she might have said herself . . . *pretty cool.*

Chapter 4

MAD ABOUT
MADONNA

The women's tour had never seen anything like Monica Seles. She was startlingly, refreshingly original. By 1991 she was easily the most intriguing personality in professional tennis, and one of the most intriguing in all of sports. Even as she stood at the center of a storm of publicity—not all of it positive—Monica maintained a sense of humor. She truly seemed to be enjoying her fame.

That ability to bask in the glow of the spotlight was essential to her appeal, of course. And if it was a natural gift, it was also a gift she understood. On more than one occasion Monica invoked the name of Madonna, the controversial pop singer who was an acknowledged master of self-promotion. Seles liked Madonna's music; she envied Madonna's, taut, aerobicized body; but most of all, she admired Madonna's bravado.

"Forget whether she's talented or not," Monica told *Sports Illustrated*. "Madonna has total control over her life, and not many women have that."

In a 1991 interview with author Michael Mewshaw, Monica reiterated her fascination with Madonna. Like the singer, Seles hoped one day to make the jump from one type of stage to another. In other words, she wanted to be a celluloid hero. "Madonna is very honest," she said. "I'm probably the same way. In tennis, you can't be as wild. People aren't as open in tennis as in acting. Men's tennis is more outspoken than women's tennis. People tell us it's bad for our image—you don't always want to excite the press. The men are older. They're more outspoken. Maybe later, outside of tennis, I can be that way."

Or maybe she wouldn't bother to wait. In 1991 Monica became an outspoken advocate of equal pay for women on the professional tour. She spoke openly and intelligently on the subject, demonstrating a maturity and seriousness that previously had been hidden.

Usually, though, she was a charming flake, an eccentric artist who was a competitive fireball on the court, and a delightfully disarming young woman off it. Whether her behavior was truly spontaneous or carefully calculated to raise eyebrows became a matter of debate. Certainly, as Monica grew (she was five foot ten and nearly 130 pounds by the spring of 1991) and appeared less childlike, fewer people were willing to give her the benefit of the doubt. The thoughts that flowed unedited from her head to her mouth often bordered on the ludicrous. Once, for example, she suggested to a reporter that one of the most frustrating things about being a tennis player was . . . socks. Socks prevented uniform bronzing on the tennis court. They left you with tan lines around your ankles, which was a terrible inconvenience.

If Monica was attempting to model Madonna's outrageous behavior, she was not entirely successful. Almost no one found her offensive. For every fan who considered her giggling monologues irritating, dozens considered them endearing. Even the women who traveled with Monica on the WTA tour recognized her contributions. She had brought the game into focus for millions of fans. She had made it interesting. Her marketability was good for everyone. So why knock her?

"She's our entertainer," Pam Shriver told *Sports Illustrated*. "Monica has such a feel for the crowd and the moment. She's not only outgoing, she's approachable; she shows herself to everybody."

The truth about Monica was that she dared to follow her instincts. Though she claimed to be a big fan of Madonna's, her style and spirit were more reminiscent of Suzanne Lenglen, one of the great tennis players of the early twentieth century. And while Monica may have come by her quirks naturally, she was certainly aware of Len-

glen's affection for the offbeat. In fact, Monica
was a student of the game—both on and off the
court. She had devoured books and articles
about tennis history. She knew not only the
names of past champions, but she knew them as
people. And one of her favorites was Lenglen.

"She was a rock star long before there was
rock," Seles told *Sports Illustrated's* Curry Kirk-
patrick. "There was such anticipation before her
matches. Everybody wondered about Suzanne,
what she would wear, what she would look like.
I would love to be like that. Everything is too
simple in tennis now. Wouldn't it be neat to be
a mystery woman and bring high fashion back
to the sport? To be like Suzanne, like Madonna—
out there but untouchable? Like, unreachable!"

There were worse role models for Seles to
choose. Lenglen, who was born in Compiègne,
France, on March 24, 1900, was, above all else, a
sensational tennis player—one of the best in history. She won six Wimbledon titles between 1919
and 1925; she also won the French Open six
times. So, as with Seles, there was no denying
Lenglen's brilliance with a tennis racquet. But, as
with Seles, Lenglen's popularity stemmed in
large part from her innate ability to surprise and
charm a crowd. In her first appearance at Wimbledon, for example, she wore a calf-length, one-
piece dress that exposed her arms. At the time,
it was a shocking fashion statement, but it allowed Lenglen the freedom to move on the
court, and to play as aggressively as she wanted.

The outfit was perfectly within the rules; it was merely unconventional. Lenglen also donned a headband at Wimbledon. Known as the Lenglen Bandeaux, it became immensely popular in fashion salons across Europe.

It was one of Lenglen's great gifts that she could be unique without being irritating. Most of the time, anyway. Between 1919 and 1926, when she turned professional, Lenglen lost only one match, when she withdrew in the second set against Molla Mallory at the 1921 U.S. Open. Lenglen was roundly criticized by the U.S. media, which dubbed her a quitter, but the truth was that she withdrew because of a severe case of whooping cough. Lenglen actually suffered from a number of physical maladies, ranging from asthma to jaundice (which caused her to miss the 1924 championships at Wimbledon), and her professional career was frequently interrupted by injuries and illnesses.

Suzanne Lenglen was one of the very first tennis players to display openly a volatile temperament and a flair for the dramatic. She sometimes warmed up in a fur coat, and was notorious for disputing calls that displeased her. She understood that great tennis was like great drama, and that she was an entertainer as well as an athlete. For that reason she is often given credit for transforming tennis from a participant sport into a spectator sport. Lenglen's appeal was obvious during a 1926 tour of the United

States, when she drew a crowd of more than thirteen thousand to Madison Square Garden. They came not merely because she was a great athlete, but because she was a *star*.

That's what Monica wanted: to be more than just an athlete or a celebrity. She wanted to make people stop and stare. She wanted to make them smile. She wanted them to point, wide-eyed, mouths agape, and say, *"There she is!"* If that made her vain, well, so be it. The fact is, it's virtually impossible to become a world-class athlete—especially in an individual sport like tennis—without being more than a little self-involved.

And Monica was smart enough, or sensitive enough, to turn down the wattage when circumstances dictated. If she was capable of a head-spinning star turn, she was just as likely to forget that she was one of the most famous athletes in the world. Accessibility, for a while, anyway, was her trademark. She would answer all of her own phone calls on tour. She would take the lead in interview sessions. After the 1990 season she surprised many tennis veterans by showing up at the WTA Academy. WTA rules dictate that all players under the age of eighteen spend at least one day at the academy, taking notes on the finer points of public relations, rules and regulations, finance, etc. It's intended for the less seasoned players on the tour; it is not intended for the number-two player in the world, and absolutely no one expected Seles to honor the obligation. After all, marquee players never visited the academy.

But there was Monica Seles, sitting in on a session in Boca Raton, Florida, scribbling in a notebook, just like the 75 other girls in the room. "I thought she was there to speak, not to be a student," Ana Leaird of the WTA told *Sports Illustrated*. "Monica actually wrote down notes, asked questions, then took our quiz. I was stunned. She also signs herself up for practice courts at tournaments—most of the top ten send their coach or parents. She remembers to thank the tournament directors and the locker-room attendants."

Could it be? A rich and famous athlete who was a genuinely *nice* person? Apparently so. Monica loved to be on stage, but she never did develop a knack for looking down on her audience. Rather, she felt an obligation to her fans and to her sport. And if some players envied her success, others felt she had come by it honestly.

"Taking an active role in the WTA, spending time with sponsors, giving back to tennis—Seles is exactly what we've been missing on the tour since Chris and Martina cut back their participation," Zina Garrison told *Sports Illustrated*.

The package was so complete, so artfully wrapped, that it often provoked awe. When Ted Tinling saw Monica in Paris in 1989 wearing a polka-dot outfit, he had to catch his breath. Tinling was a boyhood friend of Lenglen's, and he had been waiting decades for the arrival of a similarly talented and stylish young player, someone with the ability to grab women's tennis by its stiff and stodgy collar and shake some excitement into it.

Now, here she was. A waiflike child with a monster of a forehand, grunting and groaning and giggling all over the hallowed red clay of Roland Garros. "Monica is the one," Tinling said. "Thank God Almighty, glamour has finally returned to the game."

At heart, though, Monica was a competitor. She was an athlete. She detested losing almost as much as she detested conformity. Instinctively, she seemed to understand that fans and critics alike would forgive almost anything if she was a true artist. And she was.

The new year opened with Seles winning her second Grand Slam event: the Australian Open. In the final, she defeated Jana Novotna, 5–7, 6–3, 6–1, on the hard center court of the National Tennis Center in Melbourne. With the victory came more praise for Monica, who was now considered a far more versatile player than previously believed. A baseline banger at home only on clay? Hardly. If Monica had not yet developed a Martina-style serve-and-volley attack, neither was she glued to the back of the court like Arantxa Sanchez Vicario. Long-legged and quick, she could race down almost any ball, and once there, she was capable of unleashing the most potent groundstroke in the game.

After watching Seles perform flawlessly in becoming the youngest Australian Open champion
in history, Novotna was asked to compare the
top two players in the game. Perhaps, someone
asked, Steffi Graf was no longer the best?

"It's difficult to say," Novotna said. "But on
all courts, on all kinds of surfaces, I still think
Steffi is better."

The rankings would soon dispute that observation. This much was obvious, though: Seles
was determined to become the number-one
player in the world. To do that, she had to be a
more versatile player. She couldn't rely solely on
her groundstroke, even if it was a sledgehammer
of a groundstroke.

To that end she worked diligently on her serve-
and-volley game. She also decided to be a bit less
accommodating with her schedule. Tennis knows
no season—it is a year-round sport. The player
who wants to win Grand Slam events has to accept the notion that she will occasionally have to
rest along the way. Now, "rest" can be inter-
preted in a number of ways. Unethical as it may
sound, "rest" might mean tanking an early-round
match at a comparatively meaningless tournament and pocketing the appearance money.
Monica was not fond of that approach, common
though it was. Instead, after playing in the Hopman Cup in the first week in January, she pulled
out of an Australian Open tuneup in Sydney a
week before the Open, citing physical and mental
exhaustion. She relaxed, attended the world

swimming championships in Perth, and tried to forget about tennis for a few days.

Seles was fined six thousand dollars for withdrawing at such a late date. No doubt she could have faked an injury and obtained a "legitimate" medical diagnosis, but she didn't bother. Instead, she paid the fine and accepted whatever criticism came her way. Considering the way she played the next week, at the Open, it was hard to find fault with her strategy. The six thousand-dollar fine barely took a bite out of her winner's check. The $250,000 Seles received made her the youngest player in history to earn two million dollars. At a post-match press conference she candidly defended her actions, and revealed that she had considered not even playing in the Australian Open.

"I just really got back the energy to practice a little bit more," Seles said at a post-match press conference. "And I said, I'm going to come down here, and if I feel well, if I am ready to play, I'll play. I did a very bad mistake and I'm still on a high. How did I think I could play the Hopman Cup, then Sydney, the Australian Open, and then Tokyo? There's no way. It's four weeks, and each four weeks I enter myself in doubles, too.

"I just can't do three tournaments in a row. If you go to finals, and if you're going to win, you can't make it physically. Not me at this age."

Age... an interesting word, for it seemed to define so much of what Monica Seles did. Of course, that is true of any prodigy. Youth—and, to a lesser extent, innocence—fuels the publicity machine. So each time Seles accomplished something special, she was described as *"the youngest player to . . ."* On March 11, 1991, it happened again. That was when Monica, at seventeen years, three months, nine days, became the youngest player in the history of women's tennis to achieve the number-one ranking. The previous youngest number-one was Tracy Austin, at seventeen years, three months, twenty-six days. Cynics, naturally, pointed out that Austin had never achieved her potential. Instead, she had become a reluctant poster child for the perils of childhood tennis stardom. Austin had achieved greatness as a teen, but suffered a rash of injuries that brought her career to an early end. Her last full year on the women's tour was 1983, when she was just twenty-one years old.

The Seles camp wanted to protect its star from burnout, and as most people were beginning to realize, Monica ran her own camp. If she needed a break, she would take one, even if it meant incurring the wrath of the WTA and tournament organizers.

For the most part, though, Seles's ascent through the rankings was smooth. She lost matches to both Sabatini and Graf early in 1991, but on the computer, and in the eyes of sponsors, advertisers, and spectators, she remained number one.

"It's still hard to believe that I'm number one," Seles said before the Italian Open in May. "There are still some days when I don't realize it. I never really expected to be on top. Of course, nobody gets up in the morning and says, 'I'm going to be number two this year.' But you spend all your time working and aiming to be number one. It becomes a goal. And then you get there and you wonder what you're supposed to do now."

The answer is not, *Just win, baby!* There is much more to being the top-ranked player in tennis than merely taking the court each day and throttling the opposition. First and foremost, there is the image to consider. Being number one affords a player the opportunity to be reinvented, to become whatever it is that will make her most appealing to the buying public. If the image is already eminently marketable, she simply maintains it. Either way, there is considerable work involved. The presumption among agents, advertisers, and the public is that the player understands the importance of striking while the fire is hot, of taking advantage of every opportunity.

For Monica Seles, this presented a bit of a problem, for while she was unquestionably a red-blooded capitalist with a taste for the finer things in life, she did not want to compromise her image as a sensational tennis player. Moreover, beneath the giggles and rapid-fire teenspeak, Monica was a sharp and savvy young woman with a keen business mind. It was her goal, somehow, to have it all.

To the tabloids she would be a goofy yet stylish young woman who considered normality to be the bane of her existence, a woman capable of saying or doing something outlandish at any given moment—which made every day a photo opportunity.

To her adoring public she would be the best female tennis player in the world.

To her business associates, she would be a shrewd and valued partner.

These were the Three Faces of Monica. They came together seamlessly in the spring of 1991, creating one of the most interesting portraits in the history of professional sports. With Monica, it was difficult to tell where the illusion ended and the reality began. The line was so blurred as to be almost invisible. It was a measure of her significant charm that she was able to make the press and public laugh along with her, even as they were being fooled.

Before the 1991 Italian Open, for example, Monica decided to cut her long brown hair, which had always been pulled back in a ponytail during matches. The ponytail was a trademark of Seles's, and at first it was surprising to learn that she had so dramatically altered her appearance. She showed up in Rome with a close-cropped, vaguely androgynous do. Much lighter, too. Almost blond. Monica at first claimed she chose the new look because she wanted a dose of anonymity. Fame was nice at times, she said, but it had also taken its toll. This way, at least for a while, she could walk down the street unrecognized.

"To be number one is a terrible cross," Seles said in *Ladies of the Court*. "My life has become a prison. I can't go out of the house without having fans and photographers all over me. Sometimes it's scary. My new haircut helped. It gave me breathing space for about a week. Nobody recognized me. But then the first pictures came out, and that blew it."

Matrix cosmetics surely viewed those early photographs differently. Matrix was the company that reportedly paid Seles six hundred thousand dollars to sign a promotional contract; the haircut was part of the deal. The plan, supposedly, was for Monica to be portrayed less like a child and more like a woman. So the radically different hairstyle was anything but a bid for isolation. In fact, Monica very nearly opted for the smooth-skulled look of Irish pop singer Sinead O'Connor, who was riding high on the charts at the time. O'Connor, with her milk-white skin and big blue eyes, had almost single-handedly made baldness fashionable for women. Seles liked the look, and thought seriously about adopting it. But then she risked being branded a copycat, which would have been a monumental insult to an original like Monica. And, shock value notwithstanding, it made little sense for her to shave her head. The bald look, while undeniably compelling, is hardly practical for a tennis player. Imagine the reaction if Monica had been forced to withdraw from a tournament because of a severely sunburned scalp. Like most adolescents, she was at times careless about her health—even as she tried to embrace a serious fitness program, she continued to indulge in such gastronomic sins as steak, french fries, and pizza, often slathered with butter—but she was not *that* careless.

When it came to money, Monica was keenly aware of her market value. At a relatively early age she surprised tournament directors by having the audacity to ask how much tax had been taken out of her winner's check. As Ana Leaird told *Sports Illustrated*, "Most of our girls get on airplanes having forgotten to even pick up their checks."

Not Monica. If she was going to be the breadwinner of the Seles family, she wanted to know not only how much bread she had won, but how it was sliced. If the public wanted to think of her as a silly schoolgirl with a gift for tennis—a sort of athletic savant, fine. The truth was something else entirely.

In the 1990s, sports marketing had become big business, indeed. An athlete needed more than skill. She needed business acumen. She needed agents and accountants and publicists. And she needed to have the strength and stamina to ride herd over all of them. The athlete who was content to be merely an athlete was no longer admired for her purity. Witness the case of Boston

Celtics star Larry Bird, as splendid a basketball player as the NBA has ever known. Bird was number eleven on the 1991 Forbes list of the world's highest-paid athletes. His total income was projected to be $7.9 million, of which $7.4 million was salary. Compare that to Michael Jordan, who was number three, with total earnings of sixteen million dollars. Jordan's annual salary was a mere $2.8 million. The rest of his income came from an assortment of sweet endorsement deals. Similarly, Arnold Palmer, one of the greatest golfers in history but certainly an athlete far past his prime, earned $9.3 million in 1991, only three hundred thousand dollars of which came from prize money.

Seles spotted this trend right away and cashed in handsomely. At only seventeen years of age, and in just her third full year on the WTA tour, she sat one spot below Larry Bird. Her projected income for the year, as of August 1991: $7.6 million, including six million dollars in endorsements from such sponsors as Yonex, Canon, Fila, and Perrier. Monica was the highest-ranked tennis player on the list, two spots ahead of Stefan Edberg, four spots ahead of Steffi Graf, and five spots ahead of Andre Agassi.

Women tennis players as a group benefitted greatly from the influx of sports marketing dollars. If they could command such fees to endorse products, then surely they had the right to demand equal prize money. "The women were blessed by having major advancements in equipment, especially the oversize racquet," Gerard Smith, the former executive director of the WTA, told *Forbes* magazine. "It gave the young women athletes a great deal more power, and the power has substantially helped the women's game."

Thomas Keim, who was at the time director of event marketing for Kraft General Foods, title sponsor of the women's tour, also pointed out that while athletes such as Arnold Palmer and Jack Nicklaus attracted an older, affluent audience, a tennis player like Seles appealed to the burgeoning youth market, whose buying potential had barely been tapped. "These child stars," Keim said, "are teenage heroines."

Of course, there was a potential downside to all of this exposure and wealth. The road to Wimbledon was littered with the bodies of burned out child stars and their shattered families, people who reached for the brass ring and fell on their faces. It was enough to make even a tennis fanatic like Bud Collins, the *Boston Globe* columnist and NBC analyst, shake his head. "More and more people are getting their kids into tennis, whether looking for meal tickets or college scholarships," Collins told *Forbes*. "You see the kids with their entourages: fathers, coaches, people trailing the kids to wipe their noses and clean their diapers."

It didn't work that way in the Seles family, where common sense often prevailed. Monica was protected at home, but not worshipped. She wiped her own nose, thank you. For a flake, she was remarkably level-headed. And, truth be told, when Monica ran through a mental checklist of all that was good and bad about being a rich and famous athlete, she had to admit . . . it sure beat the alternative.

Chapter 5

MYSTERY GIRL

In Rome, Monica was the object of considerable attention and affection. After an early-round match, one Italian newspaper, the *Corriere Della Sera*, carried a story with the following headline: MONICA, LA BAMBINA S'E FATTA DONNA. Translation: "Monica, the baby has turned into a woman."

The woman was only human, though. After promising to take time off once in a while to give her young body a chance to recuperate between matches, Monica was back on the treadmill, and the pace took its toll. Her hypercompetitive nature carried her through to a seventh consecutive final of the 1991 season at the Italian Open. But there, against Gabriela Sabatini, the tank ran dry. Seles played her heart out in a rain-delayed final, only to come out on the losing end of a 6–3, 6–2 decision.

It was the second consecutive week in which she had lost a final. The previous week she had been defeated by Graf in Hamburg, again in a rain-soaked final. After both losses, Monica was typically gracious and composed. Or so it seemed. She held up well during the trophy presentation in Rome, sat patiently through a post-match press conference, and even won the doubles title with Jennifer Capriati. A few hours later, though, while standing outside the women's locker room, with a few hundred fans milling about, Monica burst into tears. Capriati's father, Stefano, tried to convince her to save her sadness for a more private setting. But she didn't listen. She was tired and sore and hungry, and when the emotions welled up inside her, she decided to let them out. If people wanted to watch, let them. That was Monica's way.

More and more it was also becoming Monica's way to speak her mind—whether anyone wanted to listen was irrelevant. At the French Open she once again dredged up the issue of prize money on the women's tour. Roland Garros was an ideal backdrop for this debate, since the French Open was one of two Grand Slam tournaments (the other was Wimbledon) that did not offer equal prize money to men and women. The men's winner in Paris in 1991 would receive approximately $413,000; the women's winner would receive $380,000.

"It's a tradition," Seles said, acknowledging the obvious. "But I think a lot of traditions should change."

Her argument was refuted by any number of male players, including American Jim Courier, who pointed out that the men's tour tended to be a bit more competitive than the women's tour. On any given week, Courier said, it was common for a male player ranked in the eighties or nineties to reach the quarterfinals. Not so in the women's bracket, where a handful of players—namely Seles, Graf, Sabatini, and Sanchez Vicario—almost always waltzed into the quarters or semis.

"Our top hundred and twenty-eight guys are out there fighting it out every round," Courier said. "Their top players never don't make the quarterfinals."

The implication was this: Customers get more for their money when they watch a men's tournament. Monica disagreed, and she said so. Interestingly, though, she did not have the full backing of her fellow WTA members. Graf, for example, made it clear that she was tired of hearing Monica whine about prize money equity. "We make enough," Graf said. "We don't need more."

Mary Jo Fernandez, who was ranked number four in the world at the time, sided with Graf. "I'm happy with what we have," Fernandez said. "I don't think we should be greedy."

To Seles, it wasn't a matter of greed. It was a

matter of common sense. As in dollars and . . . as in *business* sense. She saw the crowds that flocked to watch women's tennis at the Grand Slam events. She saw the advertising dollars that came rolling in. She saw her name on the *Forbes* list, above the name of any male player, and she wondered why her paycheck was smaller.

If Monica was confident and outspoken, though, she always managed to stop short of being overbearing. She had made her point. Now it was time to concentrate on playing tennis. Predictably, she breezed through the early rounds of the French Open. Then, in the semifinals, she got a rematch with Sabatini. As in Rome, the skies opened above Sabatini and Seles, dousing the crowd at Roland Garros and turning the red clay to mud. The first rain delay, which came with Seles leading 3–2 in the first set, was brief. Sabatini came back to tie the score at 4–4 before the weather turned really ugly. Ninety minutes later, the tarp was finally rolled back and the players returned to the court. At the Italian Open, it was Seles who had trouble finding her stroke after a delay; this time it was Sabatini. Seles held serve to take a 5–4 lead. Then Sabatini choked, double-faulting at deuce and hitting a forehand wide to give Seles the break and the set.

Sabatini's spirit was broken after that. Seles, smelling blood, jumped out to a 4–0 lead and cruised to a 6–1 victory in the second set.

"I made a few mistakes in the first game we

played after the rain," Sabatini told reporters afterward. "And [Seles] started mixing it up a little more. She didn't just try to kill the ball."

Seles's opponent in the final was Sanchez Vicario, who had stunned the crowd at Roland Garros by completely eviscerating Graf in the other semifinal. The final score was 6–0, 6–2. It was the first time in seven years that Graf had failed to win a single game in a set. That triumph gave Sanchez Vicario a much-needed dose of confidence heading into a showdown with Seles—the two had met four times in the past, and Seles had won every match. "This is the best tournament on clay," Sanchez Vicario noted, "and clay is my best surface."

True on both counts. The French Open was synonymous with clay-court tennis, and Sanchez Vicario was a clay-court specialist. She had, in fact, won the tournament in 1989, when she was only seventeen years old. Prior to Monica's victory in 1990, Sanchez Vicario was the youngest French Open champion in history. But this was a new year, and it belonged entirely to Monica Seles.

Still, there was a moment when it looked like Sanchez Vicario might stretch Seles to her limit. After dropping the first set, 6–3, Sanchez Vicario came charging back. A tenacious competitor with the staying power of a pit bull, Sanchez Vicario traded baseline bullets with Seles all afternoon, and at the beginning of the second set, her patience and resiliency began to pay off. Seles hurried a few shots, lost her temper with a line judge, and in general appeared to lack the focus that made her the best player in the game. When Seles blasted a forehand long off a drop shot in the fifth game, Sanchez Vicario had a 4–1 lead. Seles, meanwhile, was reduced to slapping her own racquet and muttering under her breath.

"I was so mad at myself," Monica would later explain. "I said, 'Forget it and start playing.' And I just concentrated on a third set."

Not a bad strategy. As it turned out, though, a third set was not necessary. Seles, gritting her teeth and grunting for all she was worth, held serve in the sixth game and then broke Sanchez Vicario to cut the deficit to 4–3. In the eighth game Seles held again, and in the ninth she broke again. Suddenly, Monica held a 5–4 advantage, and the sweat on Sanchez Vicario's brow had less to do with exertion than nervousness. Seles was one of the best closers in tennis. It was hard enough to beat her from the front; from behind, it was nearly impossible. On her favorite surface, in her favorite tournament, Sanchez Vicario was choking badly. Her sturdy legs were turning to jelly. Her usually reliable forehand couldn't find the court.

Sanchez Vicario is nothing if not a fighter, though. After falling behind 30–0 in the tenth game, she dug in once more, ripping consecutive backhand winners to bring the game to deuce. Then Seles pushed a forehand into the net to give Sanchez Vicario break point. "She was back to-

tally in the match," Seles would later say. "Anything could happen at that point."

What happened was riveting. The two women
hammered each other relentlessly, each whack-
ing groundstrokes as hard as she could. Seles
survived the break opportunity, then reached
match point three times, only to have Sanchez
Vicario endure each one. One rally lasted twenty
shots; another lasted thirty-two. Seles set up
match point number four with a backhand winner, and won the match when Sanchez Vicario
sent a backhand into the net. The two women
met at the net as the crowd applauded. It had
taken ninety minutes to play two sets—and
twenty-nine minutes to play the last game.

"I think if I would have won that game, everything would have changed," Sanchez Vicario
said afterward. "I didn't have as much chance
because most of the balls were long."

The victory put Seles halfway to a sweep of
the Grand Slam tournaments. To accomplish
such a feat, especially at such a young age,
would have been remarkable. After all, only
three women had won the Grand Slam: Maureen
Connolly (1953), Margaret Smith Court (1970),
and Steffi Graf (1988). And, at the time of her
sweep, each of one those women was older than
Seles was in 1991. So, there it was again. . . .

The youngest player ever to win the Grand Slam!

Monica liked the sound of that, but she knew
there was work to be done before she could hope
to win either of the two remaining tournaments.

She was becoming a more versatile player, but the grass of Wimbledon and the hard courts of the Open favored a player who came off the baseline once in a while. Even a woman who pounded the ball like Seles would have trouble on grass.

"I'll have to play my best tennis and go to the net more," Seles said of her Wimbledon plans. "I'll have to be more aggressive."

When informed of Monica's remarks, Sanchez Vicario seemed surprised. Understandably so. She had just spent a good chunk of the afternoon playing Ping-Pong with a human backboard. For all her talk of diversification, Seles had relied on her usual strengths at Roland Garros, and Sanchez Vicario found it difficult to believe that a major change in strategy was in the works.

"I want to see that," she said with a smile. And she wasn't alone. Unfortunately, she would have to wait. The world would have to wait. Monica Seles, the most accessible player in professional tennis, was about to disappear.

June 21, 1991, was supposed to be a quiet day at Wimbledon. It was to be a day of practice and formalities at the ancient, elegant All-England Club. A day of preparation and anticipation. The day before Opening Day. Instead, it was one of the most surprising days in the long and storied history of Wimbledon.

Just hours before the schedule of first-round matches was to be posted, Monica Seles shocked the tennis world by announcing her withdrawal from Wimbledon. In a prepared statement released to the press, Seles gave no specific reason for the withdrawal, though she had told tournament officials that she was having difficulty recovering from an injury.

"I'm very disappointed to miss Wimbledon this year but I look forward to returning in 1992," Seles said in her statement. She also indicated that she expected to be out no more than a few weeks.

Predictably, Wimbledon officials began suffering intense withdrawal symptoms of their own. They were angry, nervous, irritable . . . even a bit nauseated. They had lost their number-one seed on the eve of the tournament, and they were none too pleased. "It's a complete surprise," Wimbledon referee Alan Mills said—in an equally terse prepared statement released by the All-England Club. "It came as a complete surprise to me."

For a few hours Seles was given the benefit of the doubt. Other players—and even members of the media—expressed sympathy. There was no reason to doubt the veracity of her statement. Monica was one of the most intensely competitive players in the game; surely the prospect of missing Wimbledon and forfeiting a chance at a historic Grand Slam sweep bothered her more than anyone else.

"She may never have that chance again," Martina Navratilova told the *Washington Post*. "I just hope she gets healthy."

With Seles out, Graf was elevated to number-one seed, Sabatini to number two. Navratilova, a nine-time Wimbledon champion, moved from number four to number three. It would be some time, however, before the focus was on tennis. Over the next few days—actually, the next few months—the tennis world trained its eye on Monica Seles. That she couldn't be found didn't seem to matter. In her absence, Monica became bigger than ever. By not playing, she grabbed more headlines than the players. Wimbledon '91 was Seles's greatest public relations stunt, even if it wasn't a stunt. For the first time in her life, she decided to be quiet, and the silence prompted others to talk. Suddenly, she wasn't just a tennis player with an injury.

She was a celebrity in hiding. She was what she had always longed to be. She was . . .

Mysterious.

The next day the story began to pick up steam. The Yugoslavian newspaper *Vjesnik* reported that Monica had withdrawn because of a knee injury. "I felt a big pain in my knee during an intensive training session," Seles was quoted as saying. "I can barely walk right now. I feel terrible. I don't care about missing the chance of a Grand Slam win. It's just that every Wimbledon is something special, and I feel bad about not taking part."

That simple explanation was not to be the end of it. It was also revealed that Seles had told Wimbledon officials that her injury had been sustained in "a minor accident," which opened the door to wide speculation. Why type of minor accident? While practicing? Driving a car? Walking her dog, Astro? No one knew, because Monica wasn't talking, at least not to American journalists. Another Yugoslavian publication reported that Seles had not injured her leg, but her arm. Other publications speculated that she was suffering from shin splints, a condition exacerbated by spending too much time on the courts without getting enough rest. Meanwhile, the *Denver Post* reported that Seles had been in Vail, Colorado, the previous week for an examination by orthopedic specialist Dr. Richard Steadman, who included among his patients Martina Navratilova.

The *Washington Post* also reported on June 24 that Monica had been treated at the Steadman-Hawkins Clinic in Vail the previous week. The story quoted a source in Vail as saying Seles had undergone a magnetic resonance imaging test and was treated by Dr. Richard Hawkins. "She has tendinitis," the source said. "And it's bad enough that she was told to stop playing."

The *Sunday Express* of London obtained an interview with Hawkins, who said Seles had irritated the soft tissue on the back of her tibia. The problem, he said, was not the result of an accident, but rather a fairly typical overuse injury.

"The problem arises from playing on hard surfaces and excessive overuse on that part of the leg," Hawkins said. "Obviously Monica feels a bit discouraged, but she appreciates she cannot perform to the level she would wish to attain at Wimbledon. She has a lot of pain, and it would be very difficult for her to play."

That same day, the Women's Tennis Association fined Seles six thousand dollars. According to WTA executive director Gerard Smith, a player was permitted only one late medical withdrawal per year; Seles had already used her allotment. Smith was fond of Seles, of course, because she had been good for the tour. Her talent and charm had won the sport countless new fans. But Smith was put in the awkward position of trying to defend Monica, of speaking for her in her absence. But he couldn't. "I just tried calling her fifteen minutes ago," he told reporters at Wimbledon. "She doesn't answer the phone. I don't know why. She may not be there, for all I know. We would like her to provide more specifics."

Indeed, no one outside of her immediate camp seemed to know where Monica was. And the longer she remained hidden, the more ludicrous the story became. The British tabloids were in an absolute lather, tripping over one another in an effort to see which could put the spiciest spin on the "Monica Affair." One reported that she was suffering from an ulcer. Another, picking up on a rumor that began in her native Yugoslavia, suggested that she was pregnant and hiding out at the Florida estate of New York financier Donald Trump. The *Sun* took the unofficial prize for funniest front page of the Wimbledon fortnight when it splashed this one-word headline across its cover: "WIMBLEMUM!" Of course, no one put much stock in the rumors. They were just tabloid gossip, an obvious attempt to increase circulation by peddling sleaze. Anyone with a modicum of intelligence would see through it.

Right?

"I think it's ridiculous," Jennifer Capriati told the *Washington Post*. "These tabloids say whatever they want. Obviously it's not true. . . . Hopefully."

As long as Monica was unwilling to defend herself, the tabloids could say what they wanted. So could everyone else. As a matter of fact, it was Monica's silence—rather than her withdrawal—that caused the most trouble. That she had come down with an injury was acceptable, if more than a little disappointing; that she refused to talk about it was not acceptable. NBC broadcaster Bud Collins, for example, went on a tirade during the network's Wimbledon coverage, suggesting, among other things, that Seles be banned from the sport for a year.

No one wanted that. Not the fans, not the WTA, not the promoters. And certainly not Monica.

A week after Steffi Graf captured the women's title at Wimbledon, Robin Gelman, a spokesman

for the Pathmark Tennis Classic in Mahwah,
New Jersey, announced that Seles intended to
honor a commitment to compete in the tournament. Gelman had received confirmation from
International Management Group that Seles was
healthy and prepared to compete. That was exciting news, primarily because, as part of her
contractual agreement—which reportedly included a whopping $350,000 appearance fee—
Seles was obligated to meet with reporters at a
press conference before her first match. This was
great news for tournament director John Korff,
whose little exhibition had suddenly become the
most anticipated media event of the year. When
it came to promoting the tournament, Korff
wisely focused on the press conference, which he
hyperbolically dubbed "the biggest thing in
women's tennis since King vs. Riggs."

For a couple hours it almost seemed that way.
On a sweltering summer day in mid July, Seles
stepped out of the New Jersey haze and into a
steamy press tent at Ramapo College to chat
with more than a hundred reporters. She was
fashionably late, of course. And some of the excitement had been lost, for Monica had already
granted ABC's "Good Morning America" an exclusive interview that very morning. Still, it was
a sensational event, if only because it was so in-
credibly silly. Wearing black jeans and a tank
top, and holding Astro in her arms, Monica sat
before the microphones and cameras for more
than forty-five minutes and attempted to answer

every question in her own inimitable style. First on the agenda was a request for an explanation: Why had she missed Wimbledon? Really.

"The truth is totally that it was shin splints and a stress fracture," Monica said. "I never wanted it to come out this way. People were looking for something more exciting and didn't want to accept the real reason. Why would I want to miss the biggest tournament?"

Monica said she found rumors of a pregnancy to be laughable; but she was legitimately hurt by suggestions that she had skipped Wimbledon in order to protect her number-one ranking and thus earn more money from endorsements. According to both Seles and Bob Kain, director of tennis for IMG, her bonus for the year had already been established; it would not have changed regardless of her performance at Wimbledon.

Monica understood that people expected, and probably deserved, more than a prepared statement in the wake of her withdrawal. And, in a sense, she regretted giving them the silent treatment. At the time, however, she felt it was the only way she could deal with the injury. She was exhausted, physically and emotionally, and wanted to be left alone. So she went into hiding. She talked to no one outside of her immediate family. Even calls from IMG and the WTA went unanswered.

"I don't think I made a mistake," Seles said. "I wasn't ready to talk. There was a lot of pressure inside myself. I had to make a decision I wanted to make."

Even as she withdrew into a self-imposed exile, though, Monica tried to have a little fun. At the Pathmark press conference, she revealed that when a photographer tracked her down in Sarasota, she donned a blond wig and posed provocatively—like Madonna—outside a grocery store while he snapped away. Once, she said, she purchased some baby-related items for a friend who was pregnant. She did not wear a disguise, so, naturally, the rumor mill began to churn.

"The lady at the checkout looked at me like, 'Oh, so it's true,'" Seles said with a smile.

Maybe this incident occurred. Maybe not. Seles was toying with the media, manipulating it. At one point she held up a T-shirt bearing the words: ROME, PARIS, WIMBLEDON, MAHWAH—but with a line through Wimbledon. It was quite a performance, and it only served to increase Monica's marketability. Not that everyone approved. In an article that appeared in *Sports Illustrated*, tennis writer Sally Jenkins wrote that the Monica Seles who met the press was "really too much, batting her eyes, cradling an expensive little dog in her arm and affecting a breathy voice—you expected her to call you 'dahling' at any moment—until you didn't know which she deserved more, a screen test or a cream pie in the face.

"Is this the part where we learn that Seles, the number one women's tennis player in the world, has a past? That in another life she had been married to a gas station pump boy and lived above a diner? That her angora sweater had caught the eye of a major producer as he leafed through a magazine at the drugstore counter where she was enjoying a malt? That her real name was Edwina Kerchinsky, waitress? Cut."

Well, nothing that preposterous, but indeed Monica was proving to be quite an actress. According to *Sports Illustrated*, she had even rehearsed her performance the night before the press conference in New Jersey; with the help of a publicist and a tape recorder, she had staged a dress rehearsal.

Monica's reputation withstood the Wimbledon controversy. She endured a lecture from Gerard Smith and an additional twenty thousand-dollar fine for playing in Mahwah after backing out of an agreement to represent Yugoslavia in the Federation Cup the same week. To prevent players from skipping sanctioned events in favor of exhibitions, the WTA often imposed such fines. The Pathmark Classic, its name notwithstanding, was hardly a classic; it was merely a rich exhibition. Seles said she would appeal the fine, but did not make a big issue out of it. Generally speaking, she took her hits—from the media, from her fellow players, from the fans—and moved on. She seemed less traumatized than amused by the whole experience.

Monica caught another bad wave of publicity in mid-August, when she was banned from competing in the 1992 Summer Olympics. The International Tennis Federation ruled that she did not have a legitimate excuse for pulling out of the Federation Cup. Since playing in the Federation Cup was a prerequisite for Olympic eligibility, the ITF was compelled to disqualify Seles. That she had presented a physician's note to the ITF explaining her withdrawal from the Federation Cup was irrelevant. The ITF came to the perfectly logical conclusion that if Seles was healthy enough to play in New Jersey (where she lost to Jennifer Capriati), she was healthy enough to play in the Federation Cup.

The long, hot summer of 1991 got even hotter the following week, when Monica found herself at the center of another controversy, this one involving the Virginia Slims of Washington. She was not originally entered in the tournament, but when Steffi Graf withdrew because of a shoulder injury, Seles was recruited as a last-minute replacement. On August 18, the *Washington Post* reported that Seles had agreed to replace Graf. For filling in on such short notice, she would receive an additional fifty thousand dollars from the WTA.

The next day, however, Monica said she had never agreed to play in Washington and didn't intend to replace Graf. She had intentionally left that week open in order to prepare for the upcoming U.S. Open, and had rejected the offer to be a late substitute. So she was stunned to hear that she had supposedly agreed to play in Washington. "I almost fainted when I saw the draw," Seles said at a press conference in Manhattan Beach, where she had just defeated Japan's Kimiko Date in the final of the Virginia Slims of Los Angeles. "I decided last night that four weeks in a row [of tournaments] was too much for me. It's definitely a strange thing. To me it was so clear when I went to bed."

So what happened? Well, according to Seles, the mixup began when her mother, Esther, who spoke very little English, called Pam Whytcross of the WTA on Monica's behalf. It was Esther's job to inform Whytcross that Monica had rejected the invitation, that she would *not* be playing in the Virginia Slims of Washington. Whytcross was not available when the call came, however, so Esther left a message with the hotel operator, who misunderstood. Somehow, the message Whytcross received indicated that Monica Seles would indeed be playing in the Washington tournament. Before Seles even knew what had happened, press releases were circulated and a draw sheet was printed. Monica felt bad about the mix-up, but her mind was made up: She needed the time off before the U.S. Open.

The explanation was apparently plausible enough to the WTA. Gerard Smith told the *Washington Post*, "We feel really badly this whole incident occurred. We don't want it to reflect badly on Monica, because this was not her doing. Given the publicity she has had already this summer, it's unfair to blame her for this. If anyone was at fault, the WTA was."

Smith said the WTA would issue a public apology to Seles for causing her any embarrassment, and promised that in the future, tour officials would be required to verify all phone messages prior to inserting a player's name in the official draw of any WTA-sanctioned tournament. Spin doctors for IMG and the WTA couldn't entirely control the flow of information, though. The damage had been done. Coming on the heels of the Wimbledon withdrawal, the Olympic ban and the circus in Mahwah, the Washington incident only served to support the argument that Monica was, at best, scatter-brained, and at worst, self-indulgent and insincere. That the truth was something else entirely didn't seem to matter. The *Washington Post* quoted one angry, unnamed WTA official as saying, "This is one seventeen-year-old out of control."

Predictably, battle lines were drawn in what became a public debate over the guilt or innocence of Monica Seles. Columnists across the country lined up to take shots. Most painted a portrait of the artist as a young sham. A few, however, were less hysterical. Michael Wilbon of the *Washington Post* observed, quite compassionately, that for all her wealth and fame, Seles was still just a seventeen-year-old kid. "The problem with these teenybopper tennis players," Wilbon wrote, "is that nobody lets them be teenyboppers. We try to make them conform to standards of behavior that are unreasonably restrictive for teenagers."

In that same column, Pam Shriver also rushed to Monica's defense. "She's kind of played into this whole mystique thing," Shriver said. "We're all still getting to know her. Wimbledon was very unfortunate because of the way it was handled. Monica is a great PR person. She took a wrong turn, but I don't know who directed her. The whole frustration of the Wimbledon thing is that she holed herself up, when normally you can't shut her up. She's young. We should give her one mistake."

Critics of Seles were quick to argue that she had already made *several* mistakes. But they were often victims of their own cynicism and general surliness. Monica's biggest "mistake" was that she repeatedly gave the pundits ammunition. For example, before the Wimbledon controversy had subsided, Monica signed a contract to endorse No Excuses jeans, a company whose other "celebrity" models included Marla Maples and Donna Rice (the woman who helped scuttle Gary Hart's 1988 presidential campaign). It was another example of Monica apparently screaming . . . *Look at me!*

At a press conference to announce formally the deal, photographers asked for permission to shoot her derriere. Wisely, she declined. Often, though, Monica was unable to recognize the line between *interesting* and *excessive*, as she would demonstrate a few weeks later at the U.S. Open.

* * *

At Flushing Meadow, Monica seemed to be in fine health. She decimated her first-round opponent, twenty-two-year-old Nicole Arendt, a student at the University of Florida. Afterward, in a rambling press conference, Monica answered every question put to her. Only briefly did she discuss the match against Arendt, because nobody really wanted to hear about that. Most of the questions focused on her Wimbledon withdrawal, the Olympic controversy, and ... fashion.

"I'm trying to bring new things into tennis," she said. "I think for the fun of it we should create different outfits just for a few matches so it could be kind of fun for the crowd."

When pressed to elaborate, Monica said she had offered some suggestions to Fila, one of her sponsors. "I think a few of them [at Fila] were a little bit shocked," Seles said. "But, you know, after I talked to them they kind of listened to me, said okay, we will try them."

Monica declined to provide details. Perhaps, she said, there would be a sneak preview of Fila's fall line at the Open. That, of course, piqued the interest of the media. What exactly would Monica do? What would her outfit look like? How outrageous would it be?

Answers were not forthcoming. In his book, *Ladies of the Court*, Michael Mewshaw described an interview with a Fila executive not long after Seles's press conference. The executive said there was absolutely no chance that Seles would wear anything new at the U.S. Open. "Monica made a few suggestions," the Fila executive told Mewshaw. "She wanted some fringe or something on the front of her outfit. Our designers listened and simply ignored her. I mean, Monica is a great tennis player, but she has no background in fashion and she has no experience in marketing."

That last point was debatable. But clearly Fila was not thrilled by Monica's comments. The unnamed executive also told Mewshaw that there were no plans for Monica to wear anything truly outrageous or crazy—not even once. "We're paying her a lot of money and we're doing that to sell a lot of clothes, not so she can design a dress," he said. "Also, there's another thing. It's not nice to say, but it's true. Monica has a big ass. She doesn't realize how big it is and how that limits what she can wear."

Harsh words—especially coming from a business partner—but essentially true. Monica did not have the body of a world-class athlete. Unlike Graf and Sabatini, who were sculpted, Monica was soft. She had ridiculously long legs, wide hips, and a short torso. But looks told only part of the story. No one had more heart than Monica. No one had more talent. As the U.S. Open progressed—as she mowed down one opponent after another—Monica made everyone remember what it was that made her a star in the first place. Not her taste in clothes; not her sense of humor; not her eccentric behavior. Monica Seles was, first and foremost, a tennis player.

The best tennis player in the world.

Not that there weren't distractions. After an early-round victory over Sarah Gomer, Monica played the part of celebrity spectator. She took a seat in a private box next to actor Alec Baldwin, which, of course, prompted the tabloids to suggest that romance was in the air. It wasn't. The two had never met before, and did not speak during the match. Their brief public coupling was nothing more than a publicity stunt cooked up by the WTA and Virginia Slims, and Monica happily obliged.

In the quarterfinals Seles routed Gigi Fernandez, 6–1, 6–2. It was hardly a compelling match, nor was it nearly as interesting as the press conferences that followed. Fernandez complimented Seles's performance and acknowledged being totally overwhelmed; however, when a reporter asked for an assessment of Monica Seles—the person—Fernandez at first clammed up. Reporters forced the issue, though, and eventually Fernandez gave the sharks something to chew on. "I don't think Seles is very popular in the locker room," Fernandez said. "But she never was. But this is not a popularity contest. It's so competitive now and the money is so big, it's hard to have friends. Most of the top players don't hang out. It's difficult to have a friend even if you're number twenty."

Well, that was all anybody needed to hear.

Forget that Fernandez's explanation was perfectly reasonable. Forget that precisely the same situation existed on the men's tour. Here, in the eyes of the media, was a catfight.

When Monica walked into her press conference a few minutes later, she was immediately hit with a recitation of Fernandez's remarks. Like a true pro, she rolled with the punches. "I never was a friend of Gigi, because she is a very outspoken person," Monica said. "Basically, out of the top sixteen players, I would say I am good friends with fifteen."

Friends, Seles later admitted, was probably too strong a word. *Friendly* would have been a better choice. Fernandez was right about that much: It's hard to have a close, personal relationship with someone when you're competing every day for a paycheck. There is a certain tension that exists in the locker room, particularly for younger players.

"When I came on the tour a lot of players were against me," Seles said. "Every young player goes through that because [the older players] are a little more jealous. They say, 'Hey, is she going to last a year?' Then when you get better, and they see you are there to stay, they get a little better. But I still have a lot of players who I beat when I was fourteen who don't talk to me because of that reason. I said 'Hi' once or twice and they didn't say 'Hi' back, and I said, 'Forget it.'"

When that line of questioning had run its

course, Monica was asked to comment on another controversial topic: prize money. It was pointed out that her match had been a complete bore. Was the entertainment value equal to that of a men's match?

Monica shrugged. "You have a player, Paul Haarhuis, and Charlie (Carl-Uwe) Steeb in the men's quarterfinals," she said. "That's not much of a match either. A lot of times when you watch men's tennis and they go five sets you are fed up to here with them. You are just sitting there and just waiting and there are no points. He serves an ace and that's it. In women's tennis at least you see some points. That is great tennis."

If the semifinal between Seles and Capriati, the number-seven seed, was not great tennis (and, at times, it was), it was undeniably great entertainment.

Capriati, the seventh seed, seemed out of her element in the first set, which she lost, 6–3, and even at the start of the second set. She was baffled by Seles's powerful groundstrokes; she looked like a kid in way over her head. After falling behind, 3–0, in the second set, though, Capriati rallied. With the crowd of more than twenty thousand thoroughly in her corner, she rode a wave of adrenaline. Two breaks later and she was back in the match. Capriati won six consecutive games to take the second set, 6–3, setting up a decisive third set.

Seles fell behind, 3–1, in the third set, but proved once again that she is nothing if not a

fighter. Ripping one groundstroke after another,
Seles eventually wore down her younger opponent. On a few occasions Capriati was so overwhelmed that she flailed away at the ball and
caught nothing but air. Once she reached the relative security of a tiebreaker, Seles had fully regained her confidence. A crushing backhand set
up triple-match point, and Seles ended the match
with a cross-court forehand.

For the first time in her career, Monica was
going to play in the final of the U.S. Open, and,
after all she had been through that summer, she
could hardly believe it. "At the beginning of the
tournament I didn't think I'd be in the final," she
said, sounding more relieved than anything else.
"I'm just happy to get through it."

On September 7, the long, strange summer of
1991 came to a glorious end for Monica. She took
the court against an opponent twice her age, a
woman who was arguably the greatest player in
the history of the game. And if Martina Navratilova was slowing down a bit, she hadn't shown
it in the previous two weeks. It had been a tough
summer for Martina, too. She had been knocked
out of the Wimbledon quarterfinals by Capriati,
and had been forced to deal publicly with an
ugly palimony suit filed by a former lover.

At Flushing Meadow, though, Navratilova
had played some of her best tennis to reach her
eighth U.S. Open final (she defeated Graf in the
semifinals), and her effort did not go unre-
warded. As the competitors took the court for

their final, it was clear that Seles would again be playing the role of villain. The crowd at Louis Armstrong Stadium was putting its full support behind the thirty-four-year-old Navratilova. "I just wish I could have given them a little bit more to cheer for," Navratilova would later say.

For a while, she did. Seles needed a tiebreaker to win the first set, 7–6 (7–1). But the second set was all Monica. Ignoring the crowd, running as hard as she could, swatting winners deep into the corners, she overpowered one of the game's most powerful women in the second set and breezed to a 6–1 victory. "She hits the ball so hard, and today it was the closest to the lines she has ever hit against me," Navratilova said.

Seles collected four hundred thousand dollars for winning her first U.S. Open. Even in victory, though—even after hugging her parents in a genuine display of love and appreciation—she failed to gain the acceptance of the crowd.

It's common at tennis tournaments for the winner to make a brief, public statement on the court. Monica took the occasion to thank not only her parents, but also Donald Trump, for his "moral support." The crowd howled at that one; when Seles strolled off to the locker room accompanied by Trump's fiancée, Marla Maples, the boos followed her every step of the way.

Not that she seemed to notice. "I feel great," Monica said with a giggle after the match. "It's over. It's a big relief off my shoulders."

Monica's every move was now being dissected. She was one of the hottest athletes in the world. Everyone wanted a piece of her. The decisions she made influenced public perception because every decision generated so much publicity. In September she had the good sense to turn down an offer to play Jimmy Connors in a million-dollar, winner-take-all exhibition at Caesar's Palace in Las Vegas. According to the terms of the proposed contract, Connors would have been limited to the singles court and permitted only one serve; Seles would have been allowed two serves and the use of the doubles court.

It was an intriguing idea. Seles, after all, had been outspoken in her advocation of equal prize money for men and women, and Connors was one of the great players—and entertainers—in the game. Ultimately, though, this version of "The Battle of the Sexes" would have proved absolutely nothing. Seles saw it as a no-win proposition and opted to concentrate on legitimate tennis.

For the most part, anyway. In October she was fined another twenty thousand dollars for playing in an exhibition in the Canary Islands, rather than a WTA tournament in Brighton, England. The fine, according to Steffi Graf, was insufficient. "There should definitely be another zero at the end," Graf told reporters after her first-round match. A low, five-figure fine was nothing, Graf suggested, since promoters of exhibitions routinely picked up the tab for players' fines. "I think if it were a hundred thousand dollars every promoter would think about it," Graf said. "But they can always put up ten thousand dollars. I play very few exhibitions because I do not see any need. You must support tournaments. You only play exhibitions for money and none of the top players need it."

Even Pam Shriver, the president of the WTA, who had defended Monica earlier in the year, now called for harsher penalties—perhaps even a suspension. "She's definitely marching to a different drummer and making up her own rules," Shriver said. "She is the one who is making most people upset."

The season-ending Virginia Slims Championships in New York was a rematch between the U.S. Open finalists: Seles and Navratilova. As before, Monica emerged with the winner's trophy and the first-place check, this one worth $250,000. But, also as before, it was Navratilova who walked away with the admiration of the city and its citizens.

At thirty-five, Navratilova was finally getting the respect—as a player and person—that she had always deserved. Throughout the tournament she shouldered the burden of being an activist as well as an athlete. In the aftermath of basketball player Magic Johnson's stunning announcement that he was HIV-positive—and subsequent revelations that he had been, to say the least, promiscuous—Martina became a magnet for reporters who wanted to delve into the issues

of sexuality and AIDS. In New York, during
Slims Week 1991, those were far more popular
topics than tennis. And Navratilova, one of the
few openly gay superstars in sports, met them
head on.

In a story that appeared in the *New York Post*,
Navratilova said that women and gays are sub-
jected to "a very big-time double standard." She
added that if a woman athlete had acknowledged having hundreds of sexual partners, as
Johnson had, "they'd call her a slut, and the cor-
porations would drop her like a lead balloon."
Furthermore, Martina believed, if she contracted
HIV, the public at large would have comparatively little sympathy. "They'd say I'm gay—I
had it coming," she said.

By speaking her mind on such delicate issues,
Martina seemingly did the impossible: She
pushed Monica Seles into the shadows. At least
for a few days. Seles's tennis was magnificent in
New York. And her mental strength was nothing
short of awesome. With the crowd at Madison
Square Garden trying with all its might to carry
Navratilova to victory, Monica—still two weeks
shy of her eighteenth birthday—displayed the
heart and maturity of a champion. She grunted
her way to a 6–4, 3–6, 7–5, 6–0 victory that left
even Navratilova impressed.

"She puts more pressure on you from the
baseline than anybody I have played against,"
Martina said. "Because she hits [so hard] on both
sides, you never rest. You have to be very sharp.

You can't relax for one second with her."

For Monica, it had been a strange and spectacular year. She had earned $2.45 million, a single-season record on the women's tour. She had won ten tournaments, including three of the four Grand Slam events. But she had also experienced her first prolonged bout of negative publicity. She had seen the dark side of stardom. And she wondered whether she had made a few mistakes along the way. As she told reporters during the Virginia Slims, "I don't want to be Madonna. I don't want to be larger than life; I just want to be myself."

A noble goal. More and more, though, it seemed that Monica *was* larger than life.

Chapter 6

"DOUBLE BIGGER"

The most dramatic moment of the 1992 Australian Open occurred several days before the tournament even began, when Monica Seles's neck stiffened and there was some question as to whether she would be able to defend her title. Rest and physical therapy quickly relieved the pain, though, and Monica was back on the court and prepared to win yet another Grand Slam event. It turned out that the neck ailment was nothing more than stiffness brought on by a long flight from the United States to Australia.

Apart from showing up in a neck brace emblazoned with expensive, colorful scarves, Monica was surprisingly subdued throughout the Australian Open. Having promised to concentrate almost exclusively on tennis in the new year—and having suggested that she would try to maintain a slightly lower profile—Monica simply went about her business.

In other words, she shredded the opposition. Indeed, Monica's performance in Melbourne during those two weeks in January was among the most impressive of her athletic career. She seemed to be playing in a league of her own. Seles came into the Australian Open with a firm grip on the number-one ranking; by the time she left, the gap between her and the rest of the top women's players had become a chasm. In the semifinals Monica thrashed number-four seed Arantxa Sanchez Vicario 6–2, 6–2. In the final she routed seventh-seeded Mary Joe Fernandez, 6–2, 6–3. Along the way she dropped only a single set. It was her fifth Grand Slam title, and the nineteenth consecutive tournament in which she had advanced to the final.

A few months later, in Paris, the old Monica was back. She stunned reporters at a press conference before the French Open by unveiling yet another new look. A year earlier she had introduced a new haircut. This time she introduced a new hair *color*: jet black.

"It's almost my natural color and I'm going to stick with it for a while," Seles said with a laugh. "It really is opposite what I had before. But you know, it's fun."

The reason for the dye job? It afforded Monica an opportunity to walk unrecognized down the streets of Paris—or any other city, for that matter. A few nights earlier, Monica said, she had visited an ice cream shop on the Champs Elysees, where two children had wondered aloud whether there was a star in their midst. "They kept looking at me and saying, 'Is that Monica?' " she said. "They kept debating over it. I walked by a lot of people and I was surprised they didn't recognize me. Even when I wake up in the morning, I say, 'What is this?' But I felt it is fun and I think my eyes come out a little more."

Monica paused and smiled. "Everybody says they love it. I don't know if they're just scared to tell me to my face that they don't."

One person who was not intimidated by Seles was twenty-four-year-old Akiko Kijumuta of Japan. Like Seles, Kijumuta was a two-fisted power player who squealed and grunted each time she hit the ball. But the comparison ended there. Previously, Kijumuta had been a marginal player; her computer ranking of 150 hardly indicated that she was capable of giving Seles much of a match. Imagine the shock, then, when Monica found herself trailing, 4–1, in the third set.

Kijumuta had won only two of fourteen matches in 1992. She had never advanced beyond the third round of a Grand Slam tournament. Only once had she reached the final of *any* tournament. But on this day, after getting blown out in the first set, 6–1, Kijumuta found her range. Shots that had sailed long or wide suddenly began catching the lines. Kijumuta shocked both her opponent and the crowd by winning the second set, 6–3. After a two-hour rain delay, she picked up right where she had left off. Nailing one forehand winner after another, she broke Seles twice to take a 4–1 lead. At that point it looked like the French Open was about to lose its defending champion.

"She was hitting her forehands right on the line," Seles would say later. "I felt, if she has this much luck and is playing this well, then she is better and she deserves to win."

It takes more than luck to knock off the number-one seed in a Grand Slam tournament, however. It takes more than talent. It takes strength. Mental strength. In that crucial area, Kijumuta was lacking. The two women played on, even as the skies opened again. Kijumuta twice asked the umpire to suspend the match. Seles said nothing, perhaps because she sensed that her opponent was weakening. Eventually, the pressure got to Kijumuta. "I began to think maybe I can win against her," she explained later. "So I was getting nervous. Maybe that is what changed."

When the collapse came, it was almost painful to watch. Kijumuta couldn't find the court. Her shots began to stray again. She tried to take a little pace off the ball, and Seles immediately pounced on her. Kijumuta quickly lost five consecutive games, and then double-faulted on match point. Afterward, she betrayed no anger or disappointment whatsoever.

"I'm happy even though I lost," Kijumuta

said. "I played the number-one player, I played Seles, and I played three sets. I played very well, so I am happy."

A gracious enough speech, but it only served to highlight the distance between number one and number 150. You see, number one *hates* to lose. To anyone.

That Monica Seles was one of the most competitive and driven athletes in the world was quite apparent in the semifinals, when she once again fought back from the brink of elimination. And this time her opponent was a woman accustomed to dealing with pressure; this time the opponent was Gabriela Sabatini, who had beaten Seles in their previous meeting on clay, in the final of the Italian Open just three weeks earlier.

After splitting the first two sets, Monica began to tire in the third. Meanwhile, Sabatini seemed to be gaining strength. One of the fittest and strongest players on the women's tour, Sabatini took a 4–2 lead in the third set. But Seles, her jaw hanging slack from exhaustion, refused to quit. She broke Sabatini's serve in the seventh game, held in the eighth to make it 4–4, and then broke again to take a 5–4 lead. In the tenth and deciding game, Sabatini had two break points, but Seles held off each one. Monica won the match when Sabatini's service return sailed wide. Afterward, Seles acknowledged the obvious: Physically, she was spent, and she was fortunate to have survived the match. But she never considered quitting.

"When I go out on the court, I say to myself to go for every shot and give everything you have," she said. "That is how I really try to look at it. In anything that I do, I always believe in that philosophy."

Good thing, too, because she would need that attitude in her final, which turned out to be yet another epic battle with Steffi Graf. The stakes were high, and not merely because of the prize money involved. Seles was attempting to become the first woman in fifty-five years to win three consecutive French Open titles, while Graf—generally considered the stronger player on faster surfaces—was trying for her first French crown in four years. More importantly, she was trying to cut into the widening gap between the two top players in the world. It wasn't so long ago that Graf owned the women's game. She had overtaken Martina Navratilova at the top of the rankings in 1987 and appeared poised for a decade-long run at number one.

And then along came Seles, with her oddball sense of humor and her devastating groundstroke, and suddenly Steffi was number two—on and off the court.

So, on June 8, 1992, they played with a sense of urgency. After splitting the first two sets, they settled into an appropriately tense and dramatic final set. They held the crowd of sixteen thousand spellbound as they tore up the red clay of Roland Garros.

"It is the most emotional match I have ever

played," Seles would say later. "It is just too bad whoever lost. Both deserved to win."

Serving at 3–5 in the third set, Graf fought off four match points, then broke Seles to even the score at 5–5. Because there is no tiebreaker in the final set at the French Open, the two women played on. Seles eventually broke Graf at 8–8, and then won the match on a Graf forehand into the net. After two hours, forty-three minutes, Monica Seles had her sixth Grand Slam trophy— and the respect of her fiercest rival. "Monica definitely is tough," Graf said. "Even if she is tired, she always goes for it."

With summer came Wimbledon and a tremendous feeling of anticipation. Monica had clearly established herself as the best women's tennis player in the world. More than that, actually— one of the greatest players in history. In only four years as a professional she had won six Grand Slam titles. Moreover, she had never *lost* a Grand Slam final. Only one other young player had ever been so flawless under pressure: Margaret Court, who also won her first six Grand Slam finals. No one else, though. Billie Jean King was 2–4 in her first six Grand Slam finals; Steffi Graf was 4–2; Martina Navratilova was 3–3. And Seles's fifty-four percent success rate (six titles in eleven Grand Slam tournaments entered) was the best in history.

Still, she had not won Wimbledon. In the oldest, grandest tournament in the game, she had fizzled. Or, worse, she had failed to show up at all. It was only one year earlier, after all, that Seles had caused herself and tournament officials enormous embarrassment by withdrawing at the last moment because of an injury; and then, instead of offering a reasonable explanation for her absence, she went into hiding.

While the London tabloids no doubt anticipated plenty of grist for the rumor mill, Monica was determined to give them nothing more than great tennis. "I don't like to look back," she said in a story published in *USA Today*. "I just want to show people that I have nothing to hide and that there's not going to be a mystery surrounding the '92 Wimbledon. That was the first time the word *controversial* was linked with me."

Well, maybe not the first time (and certainly not the last), but her point was duly noted. Monica seemed to regret the way she handled her withdrawal a year earlier, and wanted to make amends. The best way to do that was with her tennis racquet. If some fans and players weren't willing to let her off the hook so easily, others were.

"Here's a player who is raising the level of the women's game again," Pam Shriver told *USA Today*. "Anytime you play such tremendous tennis, you make the players below you that much better. The other thing that's good about Seles is she transcends tennis. She attracts people who wouldn't necessarily be tennis fans. She's a superstar. But as young as she is, she handles everything with great professionalism and amazing maturity."

A strong endorsement, coming as it did from one who had run hot and cold on the Monica Seles issue. And it was echoed by former champion Chris Evert, who stressed the importance of remembering how young she was. "Monica is handling everything wonderfully," Evert told *USA Today*. "I don't feel like I really became comfortable with the position of being in the limelight until I was in my twenties, midtwenties."

Peter Lund, a spokesman for the Kraft Women's Tour, noted that despite her wealth and celebrity, Seles remained one of the most cooperative players in the game. He pointed out that she had conducted a clinic for children in Los Angeles, and had personally delivered a check for a donation to a hospital in Houston. She had also recently joined the WTA players committee.

"I wanted to join last year, but I couldn't until I was eighteen," Seles said. "We have four or five meetings a year. The top players' voices should be heard a lot at these meetings, but the other top players are not involved, which is bad. Tennis has given a lot to these players and I think they should give something back. Maybe they forgot, or don't know, that fifteen years ago tennis had no prize money and it was because of people like Billie Jean King and Chris and Martina that we make so much. Years from now,

I want young girls just starting to be able to say,
'Hey, look what Monica did for tennis.' "

For all her good intentions, Monica could not
escape the shadow of controversy entirely at
Wimbledon. Before the tournament began, she
found herself embroiled in a political dispute.
The civil war that would take so many lives in
her native land had recently escalated, and Monica was trying to be diplomatic. While other
players from the region, such as Croatia's Goran
Ivanisevic, had expressed anger over Serbian aggression toward Croats and Muslims, Monica
had assumed a neutral position on the subject.
Reportedly, Seles had asked Wimbledon officials
to list Sarasota, Florida—rather than Novi Sad,
Yugoslavia—as her residence, because she was
concerned that she would be the target of anti-
Serbian protests at the All-England Club.

Tournament officials at first agreed to her request, but when Seles learned that all players at
Wimbledon were referred to by a three-letter
abbreviation signifying their home country, she
reportedly changed her mind and withdrew her
request. Alan Mills, the tournament referee, then
decided that Seles, who had not yet applied for
United States citizenship, would be identified by
the letters *YUG*, for Yugoslavia. Seles was reluctant to discuss the turmoil in her homeland or
the likelihood of her becoming a U.S. citizen in
the near future. But it had been reported in Yugoslavian newspapers that the Seles family
risked having their passports revoked if Monica

engaged in any sort of public political debate.

"It's a very delicate situation right now," she told *USA Today*. "I would love to [talk about it], but I don't want to get into it."

On a far less serious note, Monica had to contend with the usual distractions from the tabloid media, who took every opportunity to skewer her. After a quarterfinal victory, one reporter asked Monica if she really was addicted to butter, and whether that was why she had gained weight. Another wanted to know whether she had been advised by her clothing manufacturer to avoid tight clothing because "her bottom had gotten too big." Essentially, of course, this was true, as Michael Mewshaw had reported anecdotally in *Ladies of the Court*. But it hardly seemed like an appropriate question to ask just moments after Seles had easily vanquished Sabine Appelmans, 6–3, 6–2. Monica proved unflappable, though. She laughed and observed, quite correctly, that "the number-one player is always going to get controversy."

An old, familiar source of controversy reared its head in Seles's 6–2, 6–7 (3–7), 6–4 victory over Martina Navratilova in the semifinals. Twice Navratilova approached the chair umpire to complain about her opponent's grunting. Monica was less angry than perplexed by the objections. "I really tried to keep it down today," she said.

Protestations aside, Martina was typically gracious in defeat. "Grunting or not, Monica is a great player and she certainly deserved to win today," she said. "I think she would have beaten me without the grunt."

But the issue would not die so easily. For years Monica's grunting had been a source of amusement and mild annoyance, but by complaining loudly—at the most visible tournament in the world—Navratilova had yanked the subject off the back burner. Other players had objected, but none was as influential as Navratilova. Now, with her first Wimbledon final looming, Monica found herself answering dozens of questions about something that had been nothing more than a reflex her entire athletic career. Throughout the tournament the British tabloids used a "grunt-o-meter" to register the decibel level of her exhalations. One supposedly measured 93.6 decibels: "louder than a diesel train."

Monica attributed the sudden onslaught of criticism not to any increase in volume, but to her recent domination of the Grand Slam tournaments. "I never got a warning or anything the whole tour," she said. "And then it becomes a pretty big issue here. When I was number five or six, not too many people noticed anything, but as soon as you're number one, it's like everything you do is double bigger."

If that sounded like a defiant statement, it really wasn't. Grunting was a fundamental aspect of Monica's game, but at some point in the hours leading up to the final, she decided that it was a part of her game she could do without.

She was wrong.

In a surprisingly quiet and one-sided final, Seles lost to Steffi Graf, 6–2, 6–1. The loss ended Monica's hopes for a Grand Slam sweep and supported the argument that, on grass, at least, Graf was still the best player in women's tennis. "You're definitely not as happy when you lose as when you win," Seles said. "I'm going to have off days like today."

The final was played on a cold and windy day at the All-England Club. Three times the match was suspended because of rain. It ended in near darkness, more than five hours after it had begun. None of that, however, was as much of a distraction to Monica as her own preoccupation with silence. Perhaps it was a matter of pride; perhaps it was born of embarrassment. Whatever the reason, she tried to break the grunting habit during the biggest match of her life. And, for the most part, she was successful. Unfortunately, it wreaked havoc on her tennis game. While Monica was concentrating on biting her tongue, Graf was concentrating on the match.

"I didn't really want to think about it," Seles later said of her grunting. "But I just thought I could hopefully start somewhere. So I felt maybe I could start here."

Despite her lackluster performance in the Wimbledon final, Monica continued to play quiet tennis over the next few weeks. And she continued to perform at a level inconsistent with her number-one ranking. She lost two of her next fifteen matches before falling off the wagon. And when the "*Unnnhhhh-EEE!*" returned, so did the rest of Monica's game.

She won eleven consecutive matches, including an impressive run in the U.S. Open. Not even a nasty head cold could slow Seles as she breezed through the early rounds. In the semifinals she easily defeated Mary Joe Fernandez, 6–3, 6–2, setting up a championship match against Arantxa Sanchez Vicario. It did not figure to be much of a match. Sanchez Vicario, after all, had a dismal 1–10 career record against Seles. But the twenty-year-old Spaniard was playing some of the best tennis of her life. A victory over Seles just one month earlier in the Canadian Open, coupled with a quarterfinal upset of Graf at the Open, had boosted her confidence considerably.

"I know that I am playing my best tennis right now," Sanchez Vicario said after her 6–2, 6–1 semifinal victory over Manuela Maleeva-Fragniere. "I am very strong. I have beaten the best players on this surface and I know that I can do it again."

Unfortunately, for Sanchez Vicario, the power of positive thinking was no match for the power of a Seles forehand. In a lopsided, anticlimactic final that lasted only ninety minutes, Seles defended her U.S. Open title with a 6–3, 6–3 victory. There was precious little suspense in the match. In fact, Seles found the most challenging aspect of the day to be the extraordinarily long wait before her match. On Super Saturday the women's match was squeezed into the middle of the schedule, between the two men's semifinals. The first semifinal, between Stefan Edberg and Michael Chang, was a record-setting five hours, twenty-six minutes, which forced Seles and Sanchez Vicario to kill several hours in the locker room.

Predictably, Seles, who rarely missed an opportunity to object to the second-class treatment accorded female tennis players, criticized the scheduling. "It's really not fair to wait that long," she said afterward. "You usually don't have that before big matches."

If the prolonged wait had any adverse effect on Seles, it didn't show. She was poised and relaxed, and her game was as smooth as it had been throughout the fortnight. Such was not the case with Sanchez Vicario, a speedy baseliner who had promised to unveil a more versatile attack against Seles. Sanchez Vicario appeared to be suffering slightly from a case of the jitters. At the very least, she was too anxious for the points to end. She took chances, tried to nail too many winners, and quickly found herself trailing, 5–1, in the first set.

"It was my first U.S. Open final and I was a little bit nervous," Sanchez Vicario admitted. "I knew what I had to do, but maybe I wanted to do it too fast, so I made a lot of mistakes and errors."

Sanchez Vicario survived five set points at 2–5, but lost the set, 6–3, on a forehand that sailed long. The second set was basically a replay of the first, with Seles jumping out to a commanding 5–1 lead. Sanchez Vicario briefly made the match interesting by holding serve and then breaking Seles at 5–2. Before her opponent could build any momentum, however, Seles bore down and closed out the match. When Sanchez Vicario—aggressive to the bitter end—charged the net on match point and caught a net cord on a short volley, Seles was waiting. She took the ball on the rise and put it away with a sharp forehand to end the match.

"I just told myself to go at it, to stay tough," Monica told the press afterward. "And don't let up because it's the final."

Monica Seles "let up?" Apparently she had no idea how ridiculous that sounded.

For the third consecutive year, Monica closed out the endless tennis season in November by winning the Virginia Slims Championship at Madison Square Garden in New York. And, for the *second* consecutive year, she had the emotionally difficult task of playing crowd favorite Martina Navratilova in the final.

As she had one year earlier, Martina played courageously. She ran down most of Monica's groundstrokes, and she occasionally dived for those she couldn't reach. She attacked the net like the serve-and-volley expert she was. For her effort, she was bathed in applause and cheers from an adoring crowd. But even Martina, as fit a player as the game had ever known, couldn't keep up with Monica. At thirty-six years of age, she was fully twice as old as her opponent, and in the end that was the difference. Seles won the best-of-five match in three sets, 7–5, 6–3, 6–1. Each set was less competitive than the one that preceded it—further evidence that while Monica did not *look* like an exceptional athlete, she obviously was.

"At her best," Navratilova said of Seles, "she's as good as anybody."

She might have taken that compliment one step further: As good as anybody . . . *who has ever played the game.* Nineteen ninety-two was a sensational year for Monica, even better than '91. She lost a grand total of five matches and once again broke the record for prize money earned in a single year ($2.6 million—including $250,000 for winning the Slims and an additional five hundred thousand for winning the Kraft Tour bonus pool). She had now won seven Grand Slam titles, including six of the last eight. For the second consecutive year, she was named WTA Player of the Year.

And she was still only eighteen years old, a fact that prompted her to offer the following observation shortly after her Slims victory: "I hope this is not the height of my career. I still have a lot to learn."

The Monica Seles whose quirky charm had captivated the sporting world a few years earlier was growing up. She measured her words a bit more carefully. And yet, she still seemed unique.

As an athlete, she was getting stronger. But in terms of physical appearance, she cut an unimpressive figure, especially when compared to Navratilova or Graf. They were thoroughbreds, with straight, muscular lines. Monica was shaped somewhat like a pear, which only made her artistry with a racquet even more awe-inspiring.

"I'm different, I know," Seles said. "I don't look like a number-one player. People say to me, 'You don't look like an athlete. You look like a person.'"

She wasn't just a person, though. She was a celebrity, and as such she was fair game for satire and criticism. *People* magazine, for example, placed Monica on its worst-dressed list for 1992. And in the same week that she captured the Virginia Slims title, she was the subject of an unflattering portrayal on "Saturday Night Live."

Like a true pro, Monica took both shots with a smile and a shrug. "Oh, well, it's all in good humor," she said. "You have to have fun about it. There are so many more serious things to worry about."

Chapter 7

"AM I HURT?"

The Rothenbaum Tennis Club in Hamburg, Germany, is a peaceful, elegant place: bright red clay courts, neatly manicured lawns, full, robust trees swaying in the breeze. It is a typically genteel European club, an ideal site for a relatively insignificant women's tennis tournament. To Monica Seles, it seemed like a good place to begin a comeback after the first prolonged layoff of her career. She had no way of knowing that it would instead mark the beginning of a much longer absence.

Nineteen ninety-three had begun much as 1992 had ended: with Seles in complete command of the women's tennis tour. At the Australian Open, several of the world's top players—male and female—were slowed or hobbled by injuries and illnesses. Monica, though, felt about as strong as she ever had. In a fourth-round match against Nathalie Tauziat, for example, she even took up the challenge of muffling herself again. Tauziat had been one of the most vocal critics of Seles's grunting at Wimbledon the previous year. A more vindictive player might have shrieked at the top of her lungs throughout the match—just to irritate the hell out of Tauziat—but Seles, the quintessential pro, embraced a more sporting philosophy. If her grunting really distracted Tauziat that badly, well, then, she would try to tone it down. Of course, it was also possible that Monica considered Tauziat's complaints to be a challenge. *Think I can't beat you without grunting? Well . . . take that!*

Monica stifled herself throughout the match, and it didn't seem to make a bit of difference. Against Steffi Graf or Martina Navratilova, perhaps she needed the competitive edge that a good, healthy grunt provided. But not against Nathalie Tauziat. The number-thirteen seed was no match for the number-one seed, who rolled to a 6–2, 6–0 victory.

"When she plays like this," Tauziat said afterward of Seles's awesome groundstrokes, "sometimes you can't do anything. It's winner, winner, winner, like a boxing match. One, two, three."

The Australian Open belonged to Seles, just as it had the previous two years. After getting a bit of a challenge from Julie Halard in the quarterfinals, Monica advanced with a 6–2, 6–7 (5–7), 6–0 victory. In the semifinals she routed Gabriela Sabatini, 6–1, 6–2, and in the final she spotted

her rival Steffi Graf a one-set lead before rallying
for a 4–6, 6–3, 6–2 victory.

Two weeks later at the Virginia Slims of Chicago, Monica still appeared to be healthy and
happy. In a rematch of the Slims Championships
in New York a few months earlier, she faced
Navratilova in the final. And, once again, Navratilova proved to be a formidable foe. At the
age of thirty-six, and in the first few months of
what would turn out to be a year-long farewell
tour, Martina played superb, aggressive tennis.
Encouraged by repeated cries of "Go, Martina"
from the crowd, Navratilova took the first set
from Seles by a score of 6–3.

But, as she had done so often in the past, Monica willed herself to win the match. She ran
down every ball and delivered one perfect
groundstroke after another. It was a pattern that
had emerged in the past year or so: Seles occasionally lost or was pushed in the first set, then
became stronger and more dominant as the
match went on. It was almost as though her competitive fire needed to be stoked. And, once it
was burning, there was no extinguishing it. Not
until the match was over. In Chicago, she took
the second set from Navratilova by a score of
6–3, then easily ended the match with a 6–1 victory in the third set.

"In the first set, Martina played well," Seles
told reporters afterward. "In the second, I said
to myself, 'Come on. I can play better.' I wanted
to erase the bad memories of losing my first

match here four years ago."

In doing so she also helped erase some of the *good* memories Navratilova had accumulated. Martina had played in the Virginia Slims of Chicago seventeen times. Fourteen times she had reached the finals. Twelve times she had walked away with the championship. This time, she settled for second place. "The first time I played here Monica wasn't even born," Navratilova quipped. Actually, that wasn't quite true. Monica was precisely three months and two days old when Navratilova made her Chicago debut on March 3, 1974. Her point, however, was duly noted. Monica's career record against Navratilova was 10–6. In the latter stages of this match, it was quite clear that the torch had been passed. "I want to know what Monica had for breakfast," Navratilova said, "because I didn't play that badly and got whopped in the last two sets."

Not that there was any shame in the loss—Seles had beaten every opponent she had faced so far in 1993. The seventy-five-thousand-dollar check she received in Chicago brought her season total to nearly four hundred thousand dollars—and it was still only mid-February. Her career record was 247–28, a winning percentage of .898, second only to Chris Evert.

A week later that figure dipped just a bit, as Seles lost in the finals of the Paris Open. Interestingly, her opponent in the final was . . . Martina Navratilova. Monica again lost the first set by a score of 6–3, and again came back to win the second set. This time, however, Navratilova's legs did not let her down. She won the third set in a tiebreaker to hand Monica her first loss of the year.

Perhaps, however, Monica was not at her best in Paris, for less than two weeks later she was flat on her back, bedridden with a severe case of the flu. No one realized just how sick Monica was until she began missing tournaments in early March. She pulled out of four consecutive WTA events— the Lipton Championships, the Virginia Slims of Houston, the Family Circle Cup, and the Bausch & Lomb Championships—in March and April, prompting speculation that she was suffering from something more serious than the flu. After all, when was the last time Monica had gone forty-four days without playing a tennis match? But her agent at IMG, Stephanie Tolleson, was quick to squelch those rumors.

"She's starting to feel a little bit better," Tolleson told *USA Today* on April 6. "It's just a real bad flu bug. A lot of players have had it."

Maybe so, but none of them had been hit as hard as Seles. And when the number-one player was hit hard, the game was hit hard. Monica missed tennis. And tennis missed Monica.

The layoff ended on Tuesday, April 28, in Hamburg. After sixty-three days of inactivity, Monica returned to the court and easily defeated Sweden's Maria Strandlund, 6–2, 6–2, in the first

round of the $375,000 Citizen Cup tournament at
the Rothenbaum Tennis Club. Seles had not entered the tournament, but accepted a wild card
in order to prepare for the Italian Open, another
clay-court event, the following week. Against
Strandlund she seemed as strong and fluid as
ever—there were no obvious lingering effects of
the flu that had wiped out much of her year. She
was cheerful and in good spirits, even when reporters grilled her about her tendency in the past
year to be a bit more secretive. Indeed, Monica
had taken to using an assumed name at hotels
and making multiple airline reservations. She
also routinely declined to release her practice
schedule.

"I like to stay where I can just be with my
family and not worry about other people, about
autographs and things," she said at a pretour-
nament press conference in Hamburg. "Tennis is
just a role. A doctor or a lawyer wouldn't let you
watch him work, so why should I let people
watch me practice?"

It was widely speculated that Monica's fur-
tiveness—which would eventually become full-
blown paranoia—had less to do with a desire for
privacy than a fear of terrorism. Monica was an
ethnic Hungarian, but because she was born and
raised in Novi Sad, a village controlled by Serbs,
she was frequently identified—incorrectly—as
being Serbian. The political unrest in her homeland had obviously played a role in the periodic
death threats directed at Seles. That she tried to

remain neutral on the issue only served to fan the flames of controversy. Despite the breakup of her native country into separate republics, and despite the fact that she had been a U.S. resident since 1986, Seles continued to identify herself at tournaments as "Yugoslavian."

Some observers, however, believed that Monica's behavior had little to do with politics. As one longtime business associate of the Seles family told *Sports Illustrated*, "They've long been suspicious of everyone. And that predated the war in Bosnia. She always thought someone was out to get her."

Sadly, she was right.

Friday, April 30, was a long day at the Rothenbaum Tennis Club. It was nearly 6 P.M. before Monica Seles and Magdalena Maleeva of Bulgaria took the court for the last quarterfinal match of the day. Still, more than seven thousand spectators sat patiently in the stands, prepared to watch the most exquisite player in women's tennis conduct another clinic.

Monica didn't let them down, either. She won the first set, 6–4, and took a 4–3 lead in the second set. It was, apparently, just another day at the office. During a routine changeover, however, Monica Seles's world was shattered. While most fans stood and stretched; as they chatted with each other about dinner plans or the ride home; as they marveled at Monica's ability to miss more than two months of tennis and still

look as sharp as any player in the world, a solitary figure walked purposefully through the
stands. He passed quietly, imperceptibly, for
there was nothing exceptional about his appearance. He was sturdily built, with a receding hair-
line. He wore jeans and a blue print shirt.
Against his body, he clutched a green plastic
bag.

As Maleeva wiped the sweat from her brow
and Seles sipped water from a large white cup,
the man made his way along a narrow aisle in
front of the grandstand. Within moments he was
standing directly behind Seles. Only a three-foot
railing separated him from his target. In one
swift, deliberate move, the man reached into the
bag and removed a nine-inch boning knife. He
grasped the long, smooth handle with both
hands, lifted the blade above him, and lunged
forward over the railing. Somewhere in the
stands, a spectator yelled. Seles, surprised by the
noise, stiffened slightly and then slid forward in
her chair. Not much, but perhaps enough to save
her life.

Still, the knife found its mark. It ripped into
Monica's back, cutting through a muscle just a
few inches to the left of her spinal cord.

Then there was confusion. And then chaos.

Monica screamed as the blade pierced her
flesh. She jumped to her feet, dropped the cup
of water, and whirled 180 degrees to see what
had happened. She clawed at her neck and back,
as if she thought she had been stung by a bee or

something. A look of intense pain crossed her face. She took one step toward the net. Then another.

Finally, she fell to the court.

Meanwhile, security guards were in the process of disarming Seles's assailant. They leaped on him, knocking the knife from his hand, and forced him to the ground. Within seconds they dragged him off. In the process, they fractured his left arm. The knife remained on the court, but no one seemed to notice. All eyes were on Monica Seles, who lay stunned and confused, blood staining the back of her white Fila shirt. She was surrounded by frantic officials, including chair umpire Stefan Voss, WTA tour director Lisa Grattan, and trainer Madeleine Van Zoelen. Monica's brother Zoltan, the only member of the family present on this day, also rushed to her side. (Esther Seles had been ill and therefore stayed at the hotel; Karolj had remained with his wife.)

Grattan was one of the first to reach Seles. She had seen the man sneaking up behind Seles, but had been unable to react quickly enough. At first, she later told *Sports Illustrated*, she thought the man had attempted to choke Seles. Then she saw the blood. And she knew.

"Am I hurt? Am I bleeding?" a shocked Seles had asked.

Grattan instinctively tried to calm the injured player. "You have a small cut," she said.

Zoltan held his little sister's hand. He listened

as Monica kept muttering, "It's impossible. How can this be?"

How indeed. Security at the 10,300-seat stadium was considered better than average for a WTA tournament. All players, including Seles, were assigned two private security guards during their matches. One guard, in fact, was seated directly behind Seles in the grandstand, only a few feet from where the assailant had launched his attack. But he had failed to notice anything unusual; like everyone else, he had no inclination that something terrible was about to happen. By the time the guard reacted, the damage had been done.

Eventually Monica was taken off the court on a stretcher. She sat upright, her sobs drowned out by the thunderous applause of the crowd. Within moments she was placed in the back of an ambulance and whisked away to the University Hospital at Eppendorf. Back on the court, a shaken Magdalena Maleeva packed up her bag, pulled on sweats, and retreated to the sanctuary of the locker room.

"I heard Monica scream and then I saw her standing and then I saw her in pain and I was shocked," Maleeva would later tell reporters. "I didn't know what to do. Now I feel guilty that I didn't go to her, but at that time I was so shocked by everything I didn't know what to do."

Fortunately, the wound was superficial, approximately one-half inch in depth. "She's not very injured," Peter Wind, Citizen Cup physician, later explained. "It's only one and a half centimeters cut in the muscle, and there is no injury in the lung. They took x-rays and there is no injury, so she can be very happy. I saw her after taking x-rays, and she said to me, 'It's okay. I'm okay.'"

That was the good news. Monica would recover fully. In fact, Wind said, she would probably be able to return after a relatively brief period of recuperation and rehabilitation, perhaps one to three months. Almost immediately there was optimism that Monica would be back in time for Wimbledon, if not the French Open. Physically, she would be ready. But emotionally? Who knew? More than two years later Monica would describe to *Sports Illustrated* the moment when she realized what she had endured; how close she had come to getting killed. It was at the hospital, several hours after the attack. Monica had finally calmed down, thanks to reassurances from doctors that she was going to be all right, when a woman from the police department entered her room.

"I just want to show you the evidence," the woman said, and with that she proceeded to display the knife. She explained to Monica that the assailant had frequently used the knife to cut sausages at his home, and the sound of the word—*sausages*—sent a wave of nausea through Monica.

"And then they bring in my bloody shirt," Seles said. "That's when I lost it. I said, 'What is this?' And it hit me again."

Shortly after the attack, police and tournament officials held a press conference. Conversation centered on Monica's health, security at the tournament, and the identity of the perpetrator. Present at the press conference were Jens-Peter Hecht, press director of the Citizen Cup tournament, and Dankmar Lund, a police spokesman.

Lund: *"After the perpetrator stabbed the player once, he was apprehended by the security guards. He has been taken to the police station. Until now there is no information about his identity and nationality."*

Question: *"Doesn't he talk? Hasn't he been questioned yet?"*
Lund: *"No, he hasn't been questioned yet."*

Question: *"When did the incident happen exactly?"*
Lund: *"As far as I know, at 18:50. In a break of the second set. The player was sitting on her chair and the perpetrator approached her between the first spectator's row and the balustrade. He pulled out the knife which he had been hiding and stabbed her. I haven't seen the knife yet, but the police have it and it must be investigated in the crime lab."*

Question: *"Do you have any information about the severity of her injuries?"*
Lund: *"They are not life-threatening. We know that definitely."*

Question: *"How do you judge the way the security guards acted? Could this have been avoided?"*

Lund: *"At the moment, we can't say anything about this. But this question will definitely be dealt with."*

Question: *"Is the tournament going to be canceled now?"*

Hecht: *"There are no decisions about that yet."*

Question: *"What about the possibility of it being canceled?"*

Hecht: *"That depends on the severity of the injuries. This is going to be decided together with Gerry Smith from the WTA."*

Question: *"Are the security rules here identical with those at other tournaments?"*

Hecht: *"The security rules in Hamburg don't differ from those at other tournaments. The problem is that the spectators are so close to the players at tennis tournaments. When they give autographs or interviews, there is direct contact, so one would have to put them in a cage in order to avoid something like this. This could only be avoided with more severe security rules."*

Question: *"Was the person drunk?"*

Lund: *"No, there's nothing known about that yet."*

Question: *"Were there any threats before the game or before this tournament?"*

Hecht: *"I don't know of that."*
Lund: *"I don't either."*

Question: *"Are there special security rules for special players? Are they stronger for some players than for some others?"*
Hecht: *"No. We don't have special security rules. We haven't ever worked with personal guards behind each player on the courts before this year. We don't have bodyguards that really look after them. Some of the ushers are educated for the security of one player."*

Question: *"Is that going to influence anything? For example, the men's tournament?"*
Hecht: *"It's going to influence the security rules."*

Question: *"Were there any anonymous calls?"*
Hecht: *"I haven't heard of that."*

Question: *"Was Monica Seles afraid since she is a Serb?"*
Hecht: *"I haven't heard of that either. I haven't talked to her about it. I haven't heard that she has talked about that to anybody here."*
Lund: *"We have to say that we don't know why this person was motivated or what nationality he is; so for this reason we don't know if that is important that she is a Serb. There can be a different reason for this."*

Question: *"Will that be known today?"*
Lund: *"We will of course try to question this person."*

Question: *"How long is it going to take to identify him?"*
Lund: *"That depends if he has a passport and if he's going to answer our questions. I can't say at the moment."*

Question: *"Is there going to be anything known today? Who this man is, what motivated him, and where he's from?"*
Hecht: *"That depends on how fast we question him."*
Lund: *"We will do everything to inform you about the latest news."*

Question: *"Are there any tendencies—could it be politically motivated?"*
Lund: *"No. We don't know anything about that. We are going to try and find out what his motivation was in order to stop the speculation."*

Question: *"Is it possible that the tournament will not take place tomorrow?"*
Hecht: *"We haven't decided about that yet. For example, we are not sure if Maleeva wants to go on playing. At the moment [tournament director] Gunter Sanders and Gerard Smith are at the hospital. Only after that can we decide if we can go on."*

Question: *"Will there be a decision today?"*
Hecht: *"It will be decided during the next few hours or later on tonight."*

Question: *"Didn't the person say anything at all by which we could identify his nationality?"*

Lund: *"At the moment, I don't know. He's been at the police station for an hour now . . . and on the court, he obviously didn't say anything."*

Question: *"Are jackets and bags checked at the entrances?"*
Hecht: *"We don't have security rules as we have during soccer games. But from tomorrow on, we will search bags, jackets, and so on to avoid a similar situation."*

Question: *"So that would be something new for tennis tournaments?"*
Hecht: *"Not really. During Wimbledon they check closely since there are permanent threats from the IRA. But except for that, it's new."*

Question: *"The person wanted to do this because he had the knife with him?"*
Lund: *"Yes, we think so."*

Question: *"So it was attempted murder?"*
Lund: *"To decide that is part of the judge's responsibility. We, the police, will investigate in the direction of serious bodily injury. It could be, though, that the homicide department will take over the case."*

Question: *"How is this decided?"*
Lund: *"That depends on how severe the injuries are and, secondly, on the statements of the perpetrator. If*

he says he wanted to kill her, then the homicide department will take over immediately.''

Question: *"Will that have consequences for the court? In other words, will the players' benches be placed further away from the balustrade?"*
Hecht: *"We haven't talked about that yet. We are restricted by the amount of space that we have, but we will surely talk about that tomorrow. And, of course, we will strengthen the personal security."*

Question: *"Where was this person brought to? To which police station?"*
Lund: *"Number seventeen, in Sedamstrasse. But right now he is being brought to the Prasidium [main police station]."*

Gerry Smith, executive director of the WTA, also conducted a press conference that evening. Not surprisingly, the questions directed at him focused almost exclusively on the safety of players involved in tennis tournaments. Smith was in an extraordinarily difficult position, for he was compelled to defend the WTA's record on such matters, while at the same time acknowledging the horror of what had transpired in Hamburg.

"I think everyone worries about the possibility of something of this sort occurring," Smith said. "In the past we've had threats to certain players in certain circumstances. Gunter [Sanders] and I were talking about occasions where there are bomb threats at Wimbledon or Davis Cup matches. You always worry about it and try to take all the possible precautions you can. But the fact that it never really happened before sort of makes it feel remote. Once it really happens, boy, I'll tell you, it's a chilling effect.

"I think it changes the psyche of everyone who is associated with the sport. Clearly it's going to have an impact on the players. Thank God Monica is okay. I think she's okay partially because the security was provided here. They did take adequate measures under the guise of what we thought were adequate measures at the time. But once it happens, I think it just changes everyone's perception of the issue. Somehow it seemed remote up until this moment. The fact is, it's no longer just a threat. It's a reality. I think we have to reexamine the way we deal with security at every tournament."

Smith's pronouncement was startling, for it suggested an acute awareness of something virtually all athletes would prefer to ignore: the danger of performing in public. All professional athletes accept a certain degree of risk when they sign a contract. There is the risk of injury. There is the risk of dying in a plane crash or automobile accident while traveling to a game. There is the risk of dying in the line of work. And, while most people are loathe to discuss it, there is the possibility of being assaulted by a demented spectator.

This risk, of course, is not unique to tennis players. All professional athletes are potential targets. And, unfortunately, there are limits to the amount of protection that can be provided. If a spectator at a basketball game really wants to throw a punch at a player, he's probably going to have an opportunity to do it. If a fan in the left field bleachers is determined to toss a smoke bomb onto the field, there's almost no way to stop him.

Part of what makes sporting events so appealing is the interaction between spectator and athlete. It's the same force that drives a live musical or theater performance. Athlete and fan feed off each other; it's a symbiotic relationship. The only way to guarantee safety is to remove the audience, or construct an impenetrable barrier between performer and spectator. And that would be ludicrous.

So, the athlete—particularly the superstar athlete—learns to weigh the risks. She learns to have faith. She hopes that the heckler in the twenty-second row is just a harmless loudmouth. She hopes the bomb threat is merely a prank. When she stops to sign autographs on the way back to the locker room, she hopes that no one has a gun.

And when she sits in a chair during a routine changeover, with her back to the crowd, she hopes that no one sneaks up from behind. She hopes that the security guards are watching, and that they are quick on their feet. She hopes . . . but only in the back of her mind, because to bring the fear and the anxiety to the front would be to admit there is danger. And if she admits there is danger, she won't be able to concentrate on her job. So the responsibility of minimizing the risks is left to those around her.

"We're fortunate that Monica is going to be okay," Smith said. "That's our first concern. I think the next issue is how to deal with preventing this from occurring again. How do we reassure the players that they are going to be adequately protected at tournaments? It's going to have a very dramatic impact on the sport as a whole. It doesn't appear as though [the attack] was the result of any inadequate planning or any lax activity."

The disturbing truth had been revealed: There was no way to provide complete, guaranteed protection for an athlete. It wasn't possible. Nor was it practical. Nevertheless, the attack on Monica Seles left players, fans, tournament officials, and law enforcement personnel scratching their heads. What did it mean? How would the fallout be measured?

"Someone has broken through an invisible barrier," Smith told *Sports Illustrated.* "It's not just a threat. Something actually happened that changes everything. Things are not the same today as they were yesterday."

True enough. And for Monica Seles, there would be no sense of normalcy for a very long time.

Chapter 8

GUNTHER PARCHE

On the morning after the attack, Steffi Graf
rose early. Because she had left the Rothenbaum Tennis Club shortly after her own semifinal, Graf did not learn of the attack on Seles until
after she had eaten dinner Friday night. She, of
course, was shocked, like everyone else. "To be
honest," Graf would later say, "I didn't sleep
very much."

Seles and Graf were not close friends. They
were not really even acquaintances. They were
opponents—two young women competing for
the number-one ranking and the privilege of being considered the finest female tennis player in
the world. Their styles were strikingly different.
Graf looked every inch the world-class athlete.
She was an exceptional player who liked to attack from the baseline and at the net. She was
perhaps the most versatile player the sport had
ever known. Seles, on the other hand, looked

every inch the ragged adolescent with a penchant for junk food. For all her attempts to diversify, she remained essentially a one-dimensional player: a baseline slugger. But she absolutely owned that dimension. No one hit the ball harder than Monica. No one hit with greater accuracy. And no one—not even Graf—had more heart.

Off the court they were equally dissimilar. Monica had gone through her various stages: giggly schoolgirl, Madonna wannabe, Lenglen of the nineties, Garbo of the tennis set. In every sense of the word, she was a star, capable of turning on the charm with the flip of a switch. Graf, meanwhile, was intensely private. She had lived in the public eye since turning professional at the age of thirteen, and while she seemed to have survived the experience with a minimum of damage, she had never felt comfortable with the idea of stardom. She tolerated it. She accepted it as part of the bargain. But she did not embrace it. As a barely pubescent prodigy Graf had been almost dumbstruck at press conferences. Indeed, the nervousness she experienced before playing matches was nothing compared to what she felt before addressing the media. Graf had matured since those days, but she remained quiet and shy. The tabloid frenzy that accompanied her father's infidelities (and another scandal involving his alleged tax evasion that would erupt in 1995) only served to make Graf more apprehensive about the media.

Their common ground, obviously, was tennis, but even that was a source of rancor. They wanted the same thing, after all: to be the best, to reign at the All-England Club and Roland Garros and Flushing Meadow. To be number one. So there they were, two gifted young women, extraordinary athletes who shared a passion for tennis. But they were also two very different people.

Steffi Graf walked across that chasm on the morning of May 1. She had heard from a WTA official that trainer Madeleine Van Zoelen was planning to visit Monica at the hospital. Graf thought briefly about what she might do, about what she could do. She had a match to play that afternoon, but how insignificant was that now? It was, she decided, the proper time to reach out, to bridge the competitive gap that so often separates one genius from another.

Graf asked Van Zoelen if she could accompany her to the hospital. The answer was yes.

Their meeting was relatively brief. Esther and Karolj Seles were at their daughter's side. Zoltan was there, too. As always, the family was together, supporting each other, protecting each other. Graf walked into the room and looked at Monica. She tried to smile. She tried to speak. But she did not know what to say.

"She is feeling very bad at the moment," Graf later said. "The wound itself is not the problem, but what goes on in her head. I told her that all of us think of her and that we feel really sorry for her. It was very difficult for us."

Not surprising, really, considering what had happened, and the apparent motive behind the attack. It was horrible enough that Monica had been so brutally assaulted in the one place where she had always felt safe; where she had always felt supremely confident . . . invincible: the tennis court. But when police began to release more detailed information—when the perpetrator's identity and motive were revealed—then the incident became truly macabre.

As it turned out, there was no political slant to the attack. It had nothing to do with Seles's heritage. The assailant apparently did not care in the least whether she was a Serb or a Croat or an ethnic Hungarian or a U.S. citizen. He cared only that she was one hell of a tennis player.

The man's name was Gunther Parche. He was thirty-eight years old. An unemployed lathe operator from Gorsbach, in the Eastern German state of Thuringia, Parche was merely a deranged tennis fan tortured by a thoroughly unhealthy obsession with Steffi Graf. He had been stalking Seles for quite some time, mapping out his attack, playing it over and over in his head, waiting for precisely the right moment to strike. His twisted reason for the assault: *to help Graf regain the number-one ranking.* During two hours of intense interrogation on Friday night, Parche left police with "an insane impression." He had not been drinking; rather, he was lucid in describing his bizarre plan. It was not his intention,

Parche said, to murder Monica Seles. Had he intended to kill her, he surely could have. No, Parche simply wanted to wound Seles badly enough to prevent her from playing for an extended period of time. In that way she would have to relinquish her hold on the number-one ranking. Number two would then become number one. And number two was . . . Steffi Graf.

"He said about his motive that he is a fan of Steffi Graf and he could not bear Monica Seles being the momentary number one of the world," a police spokesman told reporters. "He said several times that he did not plan to kill Monica Seles. He only wanted to make her unable to continue playing. The way things look, he is saying the truth."

So that was another burden Graf had to shoulder: guilt. Gunther Parche was a quiet, lonely man who had lived with his aunt, Irma Pieckardt, for the past twenty-two years. According to Pieckardt, Parche was a shy, private man. "His best friend," she told a reporter, "was the TV set." And now the entire world knew that this sociopath had a big crush on Steffi Graf. To prove his love for her he had attempted to maim her chief rival. Graf was repulsed. She couldn't be blamed for the attack, of course, but somehow she felt responsible. She felt an obligation to help Monica. But what could she do? Even speaking was difficult enough. They barely knew each other. And now, with the emotion rising in her throat, surrounded by Monica's family, she

Fifteen-year-old Monica playing at Wimbledon for the first time. (*Simon Bruty/Allsport*)

At the 1990 Lipton Championships in Key Biscayne, FL, Esther and Karolj Seles share a moment with their victorious daughter. (*Scott Halleran/Allsport*)

Monica embraces the champion's trophy after winning the 1990 French Open. (*Allsport*)

The comeback began with a clinic at the Special Olympics World Summer Games in New Haven, CT, in July, 1995. (*Rick Stewart/Allsport*)

After winning her third consecutive French Open in 1992, Monica accepts the champion's trophy from Chris Evert. (*Richard Martin/Allsport*)

Fashion-conscious Monica strikes a pose at the Australian Open in 1992. (*Joe Mann/Allsport*)

Photographers surround Monica as she waves to the crowd during her triumphant return to the U.S. Open in 1995. (*Simon Bruty/Allsport*)

At the 1991 U.S. Open, Monica displays her famous competitive fire. (*Dan Smith/Allsport*)

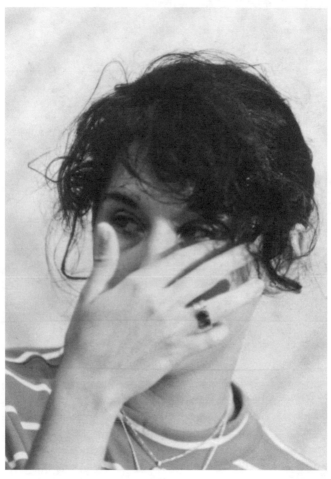
Monica brushes away a tear during a press confer-
ence at the 1993 U.S. Open. (*Simon Bruty/Allsport*)

Actress Sharon Stone shares a laugh with Monica at a 1992 tournament in Monaco. (*Laszlo Veres/Allsport*)

Despite the long layoff, Monica appeared to have lost none of her talent or intensity when she played at the U.S. Open in 1995. (*Gary M. Prior/Allsport*)

Monica pumps a fist after winning a match at Wimbledon in 1992. (*Bob Martin/Allsport*)

didn't know what to say.

"Both of us could barely talk," Graf said. "She wished me luck and was happy that I was there, but both of us weren't capable of having a conversation." It was, Graf would add, "a moment which made us get a little closer."

But soon it was over. Graf had considered not playing in the semifinals, but after visiting Monica, and seeing that she was indeed going to be all right, she decided to return to the court. That had long been Graf's philosophy about such matters, anyway. Over the years, few athletes had been exposed to as much strange, intrusive behavior as Graf. In 1989 one pathetically obsessed fan had followed her to a practice court and slashed his wrists in front of her. More recently, near her home in Boca Raton, Florida, another fan was convicted of trespassing after being caught trying to sneak onto the property.

Despite those disturbing incidents, Graf remained staunchly opposed to dramatic increases in security on the tour. She neither wanted nor permitted an army of police officers accompanying her every move. For all her reticence, Graf was an athlete who understood the price of fame, and she refused to be imprisoned by it.

On Saturday afternoon, the Citizen Cup tennis tournament went on as scheduled. Before play began, tournament director Gunter Sanders stood at center court and addressed the media, players, and spectators:

"All of you have most certainly heard of the dis-

gusting attack on Monica Seles yesterday. Maybe you even witnessed it. All of us are deeply concerned about this foul act. Fortunately, the injuries of Monica Seles have turned out to be less serious than we had expected at first. I think I am speaking in the name of all of us wishing Monica Seles a speedy recovery.

"Yesterday, under the impression of this act, we have thought about how to go on for a long time. We even considered canceling the tournament. Finally, though, we decided against that. Before this final decision was taken we had contacted the other players, of course, and they supported our decision.

"Incidents like the one that happened yesterday do, of course, have consequences. For this reason we would like to ask you for your cooperation and understanding when we increase our security rules in the future. Of course, we are aware of the fact that there is no absolute security. At this time opportunity I would like to thank our security staff once again for their quick reaction. This way they probably prevented injuries that could have been much worse. I hope that such a case will remain a single case.

"Thank you."

And with that, play resumed. But the atmosphere surrounding the tournament had changed dramatically. The memory of what had transpired on the court less than twenty-four hours earlier could not be wiped away, particularly when one looked at the bodyguards sitting in their newly assigned positions—on the court. It marked the first time in WTA history that security guards had been stationed directly on the stadium floor for the express purpose of guarding the participants.

Some players found it reassuring. Jana Novotna, for example. "Today was much better," she said after her semifinal match against Graf. "It was good having a bodyguard sitting behind us on the court. But this was a warning for everybody. We know now for every tournament that we play that we have to keep in mind that things like this can happen in the future and we should do everything not to let it happen again. To have a tighter security today is too late already, I think. We should have known about it. We should have thought before that this is possible."

Graf, on the other hand, continued to be almost militant in her desire to lead a "normal" life, even when playing tennis in front of thousands of spectators. With the image of a bedridden Seles still fresh in her mind, Graf took the court and defeated Novotna, 6–3, 3–6, 6–1. Afterward, she too expressed concern. But her message did not echo Novotna's. "The security people behind me have distracted me more than they helped me," Graf said. "I'm not going to change anything at all. We find ourselves in the spotlight and so we have to deal with people like that. There is nothing to do about it. You can always be attacked. That could be seen in a lot of cases already. I have never worried about that and today I didn't either. Not a single moment.

I walked around on the grounds alone, too. You just have to live with that. It's a part of it. You can't live with the fear. I know it is easy for me to talk this way since it didn't happen to me, but still, even though it happened yesterday, I am not afraid of it."

Graf's resolve weakened a bit when she was asked to comment on Parche's reported motive for attacking Seles. "It hurts me even more that it happened in Germany, by a German guy," she said with tears welling in her eyes. "And a guy who is apparently a fan of mine."

Most disturbing to Graf was the possibility that Parche's plot would be successful. If Seles was sidelined for several months, then Graf would almost surely reclaim the number-one ranking. No matter how well she played; no matter how she tried to distance herself from Gunther Parche; no matter how innocent she truly was, Graf would have to live with the knowledge that her ascent was at least partially attributable to a despicably violent act perpetrated by one of her fans.

How would she handle that? one reporter asked. And had she discussed the matter with Seles during her hospital visit? "I try to concentrate on what I am doing at the moment," Graf said. "I am going to try to finish this tournament as well as possible. Points and rankings are not important for both of us at the moment. If you take into consideration what happened, you don't think of those things at all and I don't care about it at all, either."

Graf bristled only once during her news conference. It happened when a reporter asked if she would consider addressing the public with an open letter. The implication was that she owed Seles something . . . she owed the game something. "There is nothing to do against these people," Graf said. "I lived through a lot even before this. I did have some contact with people like that and a lot has developed from that. You can't do anything against that. I really hope you are not going to make this bigger than it is in the papers, so that other people will try to do things like that, which I really fear could happen. There are enough people of this kind."

Despite Graf's exhortations, the wave of publicity surrounding the event had not yet crested. While she and Novotna played, a group of approximately two hundred Serbs gathered outside the gates of the Rothenbaum Tennis Club. That Seles had never aligned herself with the Serbian cause seemed not to matter to the demonstrators, who chanted "Monica, Monica," and waved Serbian flags as well as signs and banners bearing such messages as YESTERDAY THE JEWS, TODAY THE SERBS.

A spokesman for the rally, Stanisa Filipovic, a Serbian bus driver who lived in Hamburg, told *The New York Times* that he believed there were two possible explanations for the attack on Seles.

"One is that somebody has paid the guy to make sure Steffi Graf will be number one," Filipovic said. "But the majority of people here think there is a political reason for all of this, and that the police are playing it down."

As the protest heated up, tournament officials, concerned about the possibility of more violence, summoned Monica's mother to the stadium. Esther Seles, with a bullhorn pressed to her lips, briefly addressed the crowd. "Thank you very much for coming," she said in Serbo-Croatian, her voice breaking as she spoke. "I am sorry that Monica could not come. It is impossible for anyone to visit her." As Esther Seles cried, so did many members of the audience. Within a few minutes they began to disassemble. A portion of the group marched off to Eppendorf University Hospital, where they chanted Monica's name beneath her hospital window.

From around the world, there was an outpouring of sympathy for Monica. Stories appeared in newspapers across the United States decrying violence at sporting events. In Hamburg, the remaining participants in the Citizen Cup found themselves playing in a suddenly significant tournament. Reporters flocked to the site and bombarded the players with questions about terrorism and violence and Monica Seles. There were virtually no questions about tennis.

After losing to Graf, Novotna was asked if she had ever felt vulnerable on a tennis court before. She thought about it for a moment, and then she answered. It was an odd answer, inconsistent with her earlier remarks, and only served to highlight the ambivalence of most professional athletes on the subject of security.

"We had the opportunity to see a lot of violence going on during soccer matches. The security is very tight during soccer matches. The field is basically like a cage. And I just hope that something like this is not going to happen to us because tennis was and is a very beautiful sport, very gentle. I just hope that we will not have to walk around with five security people around us all the time. So it is up to us, it is up to the tournament promoters, tournament security, and, of course, up to the public not to spoil such a beautiful sport as tennis."

But was it possible for life on the tour to continue as it had? Wouldn't each player think of Monica Seles when she walked onto a court? Wouldn't she wonder about every shadow, every lingering autograph hound, every derisive fan?

"Everybody should learn from this," Novotna said. "But I think, nothing else is going to change. There will still be tournaments. We will play in different cities, different places. Some of them will be nice, some of them not. But the tennis and the life will go on. It wouldn't be good for anybody not to go on with their lives."

It would be relatively easy for some people to put the incident behind them. For others, it would linger for months . . . even years.

* * *

Sunday, May 2, was a busy day. After a two-night stay, Monica Seles was discharged from University Hospital. She did not speak with the media, but did release the following statement through her agent at International Management Group: "I want to thank all the people here who have helped me over these last few difficult days. The greetings and the best wishes I received from so many people are a great support to me and I want everyone to know how much it means to me and how much it has helped."

Seles's agent, Stephanie Tolleson, told *The New York Times* that Monica was feeling better but would likely remain under medical supervision for an "undetermined period of time." A medical bulletin released by the hospital indicated that while the wound to Seles's back was not terribly serious, she had been "psychologically harmed." Already there were indications that the emotional damage was far more severe than the physical damage, leaving WTA officials to wonder how long it would take Monica to recover. "Just the impact of this, once it settles in what's occurred, has to have a traumatic effect," Smith said. "We've told the Seleses to call us with anything, that we'll certainly entertain any request they might have. We only want to give them all the support we possibly can to help her get over this, if she can."

Meanwhile, back in Hamburg, an expanded portrait of Gunther Parche was emerging. Neighbors in Goersbach described a man who seemed "slightly retarded and unassuming." They did not describe a man who seemed to be dangerous. Before the day was out, Parche had been charged with attempted murder.

At the Rothenbaum Tennis Club, Steffi Graf met Arantxa Sanchez Vicario in the final of the Citizen Cup. Graf, clearly distracted, lost in straight sets, 6–3, 6–3. It was the first time in seven years that Graf had failed to win the Hamburg tournament. The loss also snapped Graf's thirty-two-match winning streak. "It's been a difficult week, especially for me," Graf said afterward. "I hope Monica gets well soon and gets over the whole thing."

Also on May 2, the WTA announced a decision to modify its computer rankings in such a way that Seles would not be penalized for the incident in Hamburg. Despite being forced to "retire" from her match against Magdalena Maleeva, Seles would be awarded her current ranking points average of 332.2133, rather than the 60.5 points a player normally would receive when retiring in the quarterfinals. Maleeva would be given the customary round and bonus points. "Due to the circumstances surrounding the incident, we felt this would be the most appropriate measure to take," said WTA Executive Director Gerard Smith.

It was an honorable and logical decision. Monica was suffering enough. But the WTA's generosity—and the generosity of Seles's fellow players—would soon be severely tested; in fact, one week after the stabbing, the tour's top twenty-five players were asked by Smith to vote on whether or not to freeze Seles's number-one ranking for the duration of her recovery. When the ballots were tabulated, the answer was "no." Tennis, after all, was a business, and as in any business, there was a ceiling on benevolence.

That same day, *Parade* magazine published a list of the men and women most admired by high school students. The survey of thirty-five hundred members of the class of 1993 was conducted by *Careers & Colleges* magazine and the National Association of College Admissions Counselors. Television journalist Connie Chung was the top woman; finishing second was Monica Seles.

Shortly after returning to the United States, Monica flew to Vail, Colorado, to meet with Dr. Richard Steadman, the same orthopedic surgeon whose clinic she had visited two years earlier when an injury forced her to withdraw from Wimbledon. The news from Steadman, who, along with Seles, met with reporters in Vail on May 5, was quite encouraging. The knife had bruised muscle tissue in Monica's back but had not caused any long-term nerve damage. The wound, which had not been stitched, was beginning to close on its own.

"Those muscles should heal," Steadman was quoted as saying in an Associated Press story.

"She's a great healer and a great athlete, and what we've found in the past is the best athletes are the best rehabilitators. My anticipation is that she will get back to the same level she was before, but I can't give a guarantee."

On this day there was no reason to believe otherwise. Aside from the fact that her left arm hung limp at her side, and an occasional wince when she leaned back in a chair, putting pressure on the wound, Seles appeared to be healthy. She seemed happy, upbeat. As usual, once she started talking it was hard to get her to stop. Her mouth raced to keep up with her brain.

"My thing is just to have my arm back and hope to God to play tennis again," she said. "I love the game. I just want to go out there and hit the ball again. I'll hope I can come back. I don't want to say how well I'm going to do. Nobody knows that. Mentally it takes a while to come back. But I'll come back when I feel I'm ready. I try to have good thoughts in my head, not think about what happened. I'm going to have to be psychologically ready to play. But I'm sure I'll be thinking about the guy behind me: What are his intentions?"

Monica said she had not watched the videotape of the attack, which had been captured by German television. She also said she had neither seen nor heard of Gunther Parche prior to the assault. "All I've seen of his face is just this one second when I felt his knife going up," Seles said.

She also described, in detail, her version of the attack: "I was down three–love in the set and I came back four–three, and I just told myself to concentrate and try to break and finish the match. I just leaned forward [during the change-over] to put the towel on and concentrate and all I felt was, whew, something in my back. I automatically went forward, because I knew something went in. I saw blood coming out. Then I turned back and saw a guy with a knife. I didn't know what was going on, how bad it was. I was lucky my brother was there. He kind of helped me keep calm."

Monica said she was heavily sedated during her stay at the hospital. But she clearly remembered her visit from Graf. "When Steffi came it really was an emotional thing, I think for both of us," she said. "Both of us were crying because we couldn't hold back. It's very difficult for me, and it's very difficult for her, too. But she was very supportive, and I think all the players were."

Considering all she had been through, Monica was surprisingly cheerful. She hoped that the rehabilitation program she was about to embark on would make her stronger than ever. Interestingly enough, she did not anticipate any long-term psychological problems. But then, how could she have known? Monica did, however, suggest changes in security on the WTA tour. "My opinion is that it has to be improved, that's for sure," she said. "We shouldn't wait for another victim and then they'll say, 'Oh, we've got to improve it now.' There just has to be much different measures taken. We shouldn't get paranoid, but there has to be much stricter security."

Unfortunately, there would be plenty of time for paranoia to invade her life. She would not conduct another interview for nearly ninety days. And the layoff that was supposed to last between one and three months would stretch well beyond two *years*. For Monica Seles, the nightmare had just begun.

For Steffi Graf, too, it would linger. Her victory at the French Open was marred by a German spectator who heckled her relentlessly, at one point standing and yelling, "You are responsible for what happened to Monica. We blame you." Then, less than one month later, during an early-round match at Wimbledon, Graf was stunned to see the same man sitting in the front row of Centre Court. Midway through Graf's 6–0, 6–0 victory over Kirrily Sharpe, an overmatched qualifier from Australia, the man shouted in German, "Steffi, you're responsible for everything!" Between points Graf, trying hard not to betray the anger and fear she felt, walked calmly to the umpire's chair and asked that the man be told to keep quiet. She did not demand that he be removed. Security guards then surrounded the court. The man sat quietly for the rest of the match. Afterward, he was escorted out of the stadium by police officers, who interrogated him for more than ninety minutes. According to a police spokesman, the man—whose identity was not released—had flown in from Frankfurt the night before and spent the night outside the All-England Club, hoping to obtain one of the six hundred passes that were placed on sale each day at twenty-seven dollars apiece.

"He was not arrested," tournament referee Alan Mills told reporters after the match. "When asked to leave, the man was happy to comply. The championship security guards have been instructed to refuse this spectator access to the grounds for the duration of the championships."

Because of the attack on Seles, security at Wimbledon was greater than it had ever been. Among the concessions: During changeovers players sat with their backs against the umpires' chairs. Graf declined this option, though, and turned her chair around to its usual position. It was a show of defiance on her part, and absolutely consistent with her stance on the matter. Unfortunately, it gave Graf the unpleasant experience of looking her heckler in the eye as he shouted.

As stoic as ever, Graf refused to admit being unnerved by the abuse. "There's nothing I can do about it," she said after the match. "And I don't think too much about it, either. I was surprised he was there again today, but I don't take it too seriously."

Some players did. Martina Navratilova, for example, expressed outrage at the heckler and compassion for Graf. "This is offensive behavior, and people better wise up," she said. "This is sport. This is not a matter of life and death. These people are not worth your emotions. But still, it will shake you up, because people like that, if they are willing to say that, you never know what they are willing to do about it. I feel for Steffi."

Like a true champion, Graf was able to play through the abuse. Trailing by two service breaks in the third set of the Wimbledon final, she rallied to defeat Jana Novotna, 7–6 (8–6), 1–6, 6–4. It was a courageous performance. But the victory was tainted nonetheless. In a way, as long as Monica Seles was out, each of Graf's titles would be hollow.

As the months passed, it became apparent that there was no real timetable for Monica's return to the court. On July 8, she released a statement announcing her withdrawal from an upcoming tournament at Stratton Mountain, Vermont, and indicating that she was still experiencing pain and stiffness from the injury. "I wish I could be playing right now," the statement said. "But the rehabilitation is a slow process, and I have not been able to hit the ball, let alone play tennis. I have now realized I cannot play in Stratton Mountain, and my doctors and I have to see what happens in the next few weeks to determine if I will be able to play in the U.S. Open."

Dr. Steadman told the Associated Press, "This continues to be a serious injury and the internal healing process is a long one. We work on a day-to-day basis and chart Monica's progress. This was not a superficial injury, or Monica would have been hitting long before now."

Rumors by this time were spreading throughout the tennis world. Some people questioned the severity of Monica's injury, and suggested that her prolonged absence was the result of severe anxiety and/or depression. Truly cynical observers suggested that she was hoping to cash in on a huge insurance policy. In the coming year, other motives were posited: She wanted to get out of her contract with Fila and jump to Nike; she was trying to strengthen her position in a multi-million-dollar civil suit against the German Tennis Federation.

"It is a strange experience to be a spectator, not a participant, at tournaments where I had planned to compete," Seles said in her statement. "Perhaps the most difficult part is hearing people speculate about my physical and emotional condition, when none of them have even spoken to or seen me."

Unfortunately, Monica was not very accessible at this time; by remaining in seclusion, she only fueled the fires of gossip. This much was revealed later: In July 1993, she began visiting Jerry Russel May, a Nevada-based sports psychologist, for treatment of post-traumatic stress disorder.

Official explanations for Monica's slow recovery continued to be vague. On August 12, it was announced that she would not defend her title in the U.S. Open. The following statement from Dr. Richard Steadman was released through Seles's publicist, Linda Dozoretz, in Los Angeles: "Monica's progress and rehabilitation continue. She is not yet ready to return to competitive tennis, and we are continuing to monitor her progress and work with her on the next phase of her rehabilitation. There is still no way to accurately predict when she will be able to return to daily competition. We share the sentiments of her fans and anticipate the excitement we will feel when she once again achieves her maximum potential and is able to return to the court."

Even Monica herself was somewhat evasive during an interview with ABC's Diane Sawyer later that month. The interview was part of the August 26 edition of *PrimeTime Live*. In it, Monica declined to say when she would return. She said she still suffered from physical pain, which prevented her from practicing. "I haven't hit the ball for a long time and . . . I mean, for me to get back to any level is going to take a lot of hours," Seles said. "I think as soon as I'll be able to physically swing a racquet and hit a ball, I'm going to go out there and swing it. And I'm going to practice hard. But I think for me, I'm going to have to deal with it emotionally, also."

Increasingly, it seemed, that was Monica's biggest challenge: to overcome the fear of another assault, and to accept the fact that she did not have complete control of her life—that she could be a victim. "I was always a strong person mentally, and this is just another hurdle that I just have to jump over," she told Sawyer. "It's just hard to understand why a person would stab another person for that person to be number one, on the tennis court, while I'm playing. I mean, I was in a match. That, to me, is the hardest thing to understand."

Four days later Monica surfaced again, this time in New York, where she made an appearance at the Arthur Ashe Tennis Challenge, an exhibition to benefit the late tennis star's Foundation for the Defeat of AIDS. Monica sat with Ashe's widow, Jeanne, and daughter, Camera. She signed autographs and waved to the thirteen thousand fans in attendance. She even shared a hug and a kiss with Jennifer Capriati. The next day she met with the media and explained, as she had in her *PrimeTime Live* interview, that she was still suffering from a variety of physical ailments. Her shoulder throbbed when she tried to swing a racquet. She had numbness in her hand. And, once again, she admitted to feeling a bit anxious about coming back. She also expressed disappointment with the WTA over losing her number-one ranking, and with Graf, who had neither phoned nor written in months.

Still, Monica tried to put the best face on the situation. She was a fighter. She was a competitor. She would be back. Eventually. Perhaps in

the fall there would be cause for optimism. In
the fall Gunther Parche would go trial. Soon he
would be locked away in some German prison.
And then Monica Seles could rest easy. Then she
could go back to work.

But it didn't work out that way. On October
13, in Hamburg, Germany, at the conclusion of
a highly publicized trial, Gunther Parche was
found guilty of stabbing Monica Seles. Unfortunately, the charge he faced was not attempted
murder, as first reported. Nor was it the attempted manslaughter charge sought by the
prosecution. Instead, Parche was charged only
with "causing grievous bodily harm." Hamburg
District Court Judge Elke Bosse—saying the attack was "something that happens every day in
St. Pauli," a rough neighborhood in Hamburg—
then gave Parche a suspended two-year sentence. She defended the sentence by saying that
she believed not only Parche's contention that he
intended merely to disable Seles, but also his
promise not to hurt anyone else in the future.
She was also strongly influenced by a court-
appointed psychiatrist's opinion that Parche was
mentally deficient.

News of the sentence was met with anger
throughout Germany and Europe. *Bild*, Germany's largest newspaper, carried this headline the
day after the trial concluded: SCANDALOUS VER-
DICT! THE WHOLE WORLD IS SHOCKED!

When word of the verdict reached the Seles
family, Monica was understandably outraged.

"What kind of message does this send to the world?" she said in a statement released through International Management Group. "Mr. Parche has admitted that he stalked me, then he stabbed me once and attempted to stab me a second time. And now the court has said he does not have to go to jail for premeditated crime. He gets to go back to his life, but I can't because I am still recovering from this attack, which could have killed me."

Martina Navratilova, who was playing at a tournament in Filderstadt, Germany, at the time, also expressed anger at the sentence. "You guys need some serious help with the laws here in Germany," Navratilova told *The New York Times*. "Forget the fact it was Monica Seles, it has cost her millions of dollars, and it was done on national television. When one human being can stab another with the intent of seriously injuring him, and they walk away, then there is something wrong with the law."

Even Gunther Parche was surprised. He had testified during his trial that he had planned the attack for some time, and fully expected to spend ten to fifteen years in prison afterward.

The prosecution was quick to point out that its case was severely weakened by a lack of cooperation from Seles herself. First, she refused to testify at the trial, even though her presence may well have influenced the judge. Second, even though prosecutors requested Seles's medical records several months earlier, she was extremely late in granting their release. In fact, the information did not arrive in the prosecutor's office until the day before the trial began.

Still, Parche was convicted of a crime, and the punishment for that crime ranged from a maximum of five years in prison to . . . no time in prison. Bosse chose to be lenient. She released Gunther Parche. Interestingly, though, he opted for one additional night in jail. No official explanation was given; reportedly, though, Parche feared retribution from those who disagreed with the sentence.

On November 11 the Women's Tennis Association announced that it had retained the services of a prominent Hamburg attorney to "ensure that an appeal of the Hamburg court's judgment is vigorously pursued by the prosecutor . . . and to see that the assailant serves a significant period of incarceration commensurate with the viciousness and lawlessness of his act."

In the meantime, Monica Seles remained in hiding at her Sarasota estate. And Gunther Parche remained a free man.

Chapter 9

POST-TRAUMATIC STRESS

As the new year broke, there were indications that Monica might be on the verge of a comeback. Her rehabilitation had been progressing smoothly. She was young and strong and in superb health. And, of course, she was a competitor, which was another factor in her favor.

From May through September of 1993 Monica had lived primarily in a hotel in Vail, Colorado, so that she could work with the physicians and therapists at Dr. Steadman's clinic.

"I did a lot—and I mean a *lot*—of stretching," Seles told *Tennis* magazine in the spring of 1994. "The people there worked gently on 'pressure points' in my back and shoulder, and kept me in good general shape with programs on the treadmill and StairMaster. I didn't like these programs much—I mean, how much TV can you watch while you're working out? So I took up hiking for general fitness. I even went on a few camping trips and did a little fly-fishing."

By the middle of the summer Monica had nearly full range of motion, but the muscles had atrophied somewhat, so she began working out with weights to strengthen her arm, back, and shoulder. During this period she concentrated exclusively on overall fitness, perhaps for the first time in her life. She did not even pick up a racquet until September, when her doctor set up a net in his office and allowed her to take a couple of easy strokes. It was merely a test to determine whether Monica still had any pain. And she did—just a twinge, really, but enough to prompt Steadman to delay her return to the court for a few more weeks.

Finally, about three weeks after the '93 U.S. Open, Monica started working out with a racquet. At first, the training was light: She strolled onto a court with her father, just as she had years earlier, when she was a child first learning to play, and tried to concentrate on swinging the racquet in smooth, fluid strokes as Karolj gently tossed balls over the net. "At first I got mad because that seemed like an insult," Monica told *Tennis.* "He was very patient and I wasn't, but he reminded me that I was in a similar position in 1984, when I had to take off six months because of a condition called Osgood-Schlatter's disease, which comes from growing too fast. Later, when I hit regularly, I experienced some frustration. I was used to the ball going where I wanted to hit it, but I was still rusty."

Rust was only part of the problem. Apparently, Monica did not know her own strength. In addition to her sessions on the court and in the physical therapist's office, she had also found a formidable training partner: former Olympic sprint champion Jackie Joyner-Kersee. The women occasionally trained together under the expert eye of Jackie's husband, the respected sprint coach Bob Kersee. "You would think that it would be intimidating to work out with Jackie, but she's the most down-to-earth person on earth," Monica said. "At the same time, being anywhere near her is inspiring. I mean, I'd glance at her and think, Well, if *she* can force herself to do another sit-up, I can too."

The iron will that had made Seles the youngest number one–ranked player in history appeared to be as firm as ever. By late fall she was practicing just about every day. Though she had committed to nothing, she seemed poised to return to competition. But then her world began to unravel again.

First came the health problems of her father. Karolj Seles underwent surgery for prostate cancer in December 1993. At first, Monica seemed to handle the emotional trauma of that event surprisingly well. On several fronts there were indications that her return to tennis was imminent. Pam Shriver, for example, told reporters in early January of a recent telephone conversation in which Monica had said she was considering playing in Australia. At about that same time,

Geoff Pollard, the president of Tennis Australia, also indicated there was a reasonable chance Monica would begin her comeback at the Australian Open. Fila clothing was so excited by this news that it reportedly spent more than three million dollars to design and market a new line of Monica Seles clothing.

The rumor mill, once again, chugged along. Would she or wouldn't she? The answer came late on January 6, 1994, when Seles released a statement announcing that she would not be playing in the Australian Open. The timing was, as always, impeccable. Earlier that day another prominent female athlete, figure skater Nancy Kerrigan, had been whacked on the knee by an unknown assailant while practicing for the U.S. nationals in Detroit. At the time, the assault on Kerrigan appeared to be another senseless act of violence perpetrated by a demented fan. It turned out to be a badly executed "hit" intended to knock Kerrigan out of Olympic competition and improve the chances of her chief rival, Tonya Harding. Either way, the similarities between the two incidents were striking: a famous female athlete brutally assaulted; a solitary male making a mockery of the notion that an athlete is guaranteed sanctuary on the field of play.

Seles would later maintain that the timing was mere coincidence; that despite reportedly calling a friend after witnessing news reports of the attack on Kerrigan and saying, "it happened again," her decision to skip the Australian Open was unrelated. As Monica would later explain to *Sports Illustrated,* it was during this period that she began to slip into something of a depression. She was dealing with so much: the illness of her beloved father; the emotional scars of her attack; nagging doubts about whether she would be capable of returning to top form; grand philosophical questions about the meaning of life and the importance of tennis in that life.

Monica had been working hard for months, so she took a break over the holidays. She wanted to rest her mind and body, but instead found herself obsessing about the darker side of life in general, and the incident in Hamburg in particular. "All these memories started coming back," she said. "And it just went into this tailspin, spinning and spinning and the ball was getting bigger and bigger so that I couldn't sleep at all. I would be up all night in my room, just sitting. In the dark or light, I didn't feel comfortable leaving the house. Total depression. I was just reliving that moment."

Her competitive nature notwithstanding, Monica had always been a sensitive, gentle person. She was an athlete with an artist's sensibilities, and when she saw cruelty and injustice, it troubled her deeply. There had to be a *reason* for everything, including her own suffering. The possibility that life was utterly random, and inherently unfair, was too much for Monica to handle. She could not accept the notion that Gunther Parche wanted to hurt her, that he believed, in some twisted way, that she *deserved* to be injured. When confronted with evil, Monica reacted with an almost childlike naivete. *Why?* she kept saying. *Why would anyone want to harm me?* There was no answer. No explanation that made sense.

As her psychologist would later testify at Parche's retrial, "She constantly asks herself if she did something wrong to deserve the attack." She had done nothing, of course. She was merely a victim. And for Monica Seles, who sought nothing so much as control over her life, that was a difficult truth to acknowledge.

She retreated into herself. She hid behind the walls of her massive Sarasota estate like a bird in a cage, as she would later describe it. Some days she would play tennis. Some days she wouldn't. Some days the fog would lift and she would feel like herself again—happy, driven, confident. Other days she could scarcely summon the energy and courage to get out of bed. As she told *Sports Illustrated*'s S.L. Price in a 1995 interview, some of the most awkward moments came when she was with friends and family. They would be together, sharing dinner, and someone would make the mistake of telling Monica how much the game missed her and needed her. "I would have to go into the bathroom and cry and say, 'Why am I not playing?'" Monica recalled. "Then I come back and everybody sees me teary-eyed: Poor Monica. I didn't know how to deal with it."

The sessions with Jerry Russel May helped.

They talked nearly every day by phone; sometimes she would hop on a plane and fly to May's
Reno office to meet with him in person. She
talked at length with other victims of violent
crime. They shared their stories, their anguish.
They talked about their fears. Monica discovered
that these people—strangers—could help her in
a way that even her closest friends and family
members could not. They knew what she was
going through. They had experienced similar
trauma. They, too, had bolted up in the middle
of the night, sweating, hearts racing, terrible images burning in their minds.

They *understood.*

"There were and are people I can call if I wake
up at two in the morning and have a problem,"
Monica told *Tennis* magazine. "And now there
are people who can call me if they want. They
aren't celebrities or anything like that, just people who share one thing—having been stabbed.
And they really helped me to deal with my situation."

The recovery was slow. First, Monica had to
overcome the fear. She had to accept the fact that
life was risky—for everyone. She had to stop
blaming herself. It wouldn't be easy.

"Why was it me?" she told *Sports Illustrated.*
"I didn't think at age nineteen I would have to
deal with this: I was playing, and suddenly I
wasn't playing, and it changed my daily life.
And all these emotions I didn't know how I
could feel. *How do I want to live my life?* You have

to decide: If you live till ninety living this way, do you really want to live? Why do I have to face these questions? This is supposed to be fun, and here I am thinking about life-or-death issues. This guy stabbed me, he's out there, he can come to any tennis tournament, any place. And he's still obsessed. *What will it take for him not to do it again?''*

Although she remained in seclusion throughout 1994 and granted virtually no access to the media, Monica did conduct one lengthy interview with Peter Bodo, a senior writer for *Tennis* magazine. The story, which included a first-person account of Monica's rehabilitation, was published in March 1994. In it, Monica addressed numerous philosophical and psychological issues. Physically, she admitted, she was ready to return to competition. Emotionally, however, she was not.

And it wasn't just the attack that delayed her comeback. For the first time in her young life, Monica was stepping back ... measuring ... assessing ... taking stock. Serious, and probably healthy, introspection consumed much of her mental energy. Tennis had always been her life. But now she wondered whether she had been too focused, too oblivious to other matters. She wanted to play again, because she still loved the game. But she wanted to make sure her motivation for returning was true. And she wanted the timing to be right.

"I've watched myself on tape," she told *Ten-*

nis. "And I always looked very emotional, very focused, and totally into what is happening on the court. But even though I see myself, I do not recognize myself, because that isn't really me— it's just a part of me, a part that I call my 'second personality.' And I don't know if that second personality will ever come out again in that way, because at the time that I was stabbed, I was living a very different life. In some ways it was a very closed-off life.

"I've had a lot of time to think since that day, and a lot of time to decide what my priorities are. And I decided that I want to live the rest of my life happy with what I'm doing. So when I play tennis again, I have to play it for the right reason. I don't want to play to get my number-one ranking back. I don't want to play for the attention, or to earn more. I don't even want to play because the world wants to see me do it, even though it's nice to know that the world is interested. I only want to play because I love the game, which is the reason I began to play at age seven in the first place.

"The only 'right' time for me to play again is when I can see myself and think only this: Gosh, I'm happy again; this is fun. I have to live for the day, and not worry about or try to know what tomorrow brings. Before I was stabbed, I always lived for tomorrow—my next match, my next tournament. But if I've learned one thing from all that's happened to me, it's that if you would know what tomorrow brings, you may not want to live it."

The fear that gripped Monica—that prompted nightmares featuring Gunther Parche and made her question her own desire and ability—began to melt away. Her recovery, however, manifested itself in an unusual way. She still felt no urgent need to return to the tennis court, but she *did* feel compelled to begin living life on its own terms. Professional athletes, by necessity, are often as cautious off the field as they are courageous and aggressive on it. They must protect their bodies, for the slightest injury can lead to inactivity, which can lead to financial difficulty. Few things are more disturbing to the owner or coach of a professional sports franchise than the news that one of his star athletes was hang gliding or mountain climbing on his day off. Similarly, sponsors get queasy when they hear that one of their premier tennis players has been experimenting with alternative forms of recreation.

Monica had always lived according to those unwritten rules. She was the family meal ticket. She was a tennis star. Even as a child she had obligations, responsibilities. Suddenly, though, she was on the sideline. She was not a player. On February 14, 1994, her name was dropped from the WTA computer rankings. In order to maintain a ranking, a player must participate in at least three tournaments over a twelve-month period; Seles had played in only two events, so

... she slipped into oblivion. Unofficially, at least, she was no longer a professional tennis player. She was a spectator. So, she reasoned, why not do some of those things that normal people do?

"One of the big changes in me is that I'm not that cautious anymore," Monica told *Tennis* magazine. "I guess that's ironic because I heard all the rumors about how I was in a mental institution, how I was an emotional wreck. But it's almost like the opposite is true. I don't spend any time looking over my shoulder. In fact, now I'm less afraid to try lots of the things I never had a chance to do. I don't think I'll ever think about going skiing, or ice skating, and then just shut out the idea because I might fall and get hurt. I just don't worry about things like that anymore."

Maybe not. But she acknowledged that gathering the strength to go downhill skiing was much easier than summoning the courage to sit with her back to a crowd at a tennis match. "It does go through my mind," Monica said. "And it's bound to go through my mind even more when I step on a tennis court: The guy who attacked me got what he wanted [Steffi Graf's ascent to number one in the computer rankings], and he was let out, free. No matter how you look at it, the message sent by that is that what he did to me was okay. I think anybody in my situation could have a big problem with that, which is why I don't want to play until I'm really clear on all of that."

At the same time, Monica knew that she still loved playing tennis. In addition to her workouts with Jackie Joyner-Kersee and Bob Kersee and her physical therapy, there were many days when she spent hours on the courts outside her home, swatting hundreds of balls at an imaginary opponent. Admittedly, her training was not nearly as intense as it had been in the past. Typically, Monica hit with her father or Zoltan. Then, in the week leading up to a tournament, she would recruit a male player to work out with her. They would rally for hours, Monica running down every shot he had, grunting and pummeling the ball back to him, until one of them—usually the sparring partner—ran out of gas.

Now, the approach was different. Occasionally she hit with Zoltan or Karolj, but just as often the workouts were solitary. And, always, they were held in private, which, of course, only added to the mystery surrounding her comeback. "I haven't felt that I want to show people what I have, because I don't want them to compare it to my previous level," Monica told *Tennis* magazine. "I'm not on any kind of schedule. I may work out twice in one day, and the next day I may not hit a ball. It all depends on what I want to do, and how I feel."

In general, Monica said, she was committed to a holistic approach to training. Physical fitness

had always been a byproduct of her obsession
with the game: She played so often, and so hard,
that she couldn't help but be in reasonably good
shape. But she had never really embraced any
cutting-edge training techniques. Whereas most
athletes in the 1990s understood the importance
of nutrition and weight training, Monica rarely
gave any thought to her diet, and rarely lifted
anything heavier than a tennis racquet.

She could get away with this because she was
a spectacularly gifted athlete. And because she
was so young; her body was resilient. Now,
though, she was maturing. She was growing.
and, for the first time in her life, she realized how
fragile her body really was, how quickly an injury could change everything. Monica wanted to
be a stronger, more complete tennis player. She
acknowledged occasionally looking enviously at
Martina Navratilova and Steffi Graf. More often
than not, when she played either of those
women, Monica won. Still, she wondered if she
was missing something, if she was cheating herself.

"The thrust of my workouts has been toward
the physical, the effort to become a better athlete," she told *Tennis*. "I go to the gym regularly,
for an hour a day, three days a week. I'm more
careful about what I'm eating. There is definitely
something in me that I haven't tapped. I look at
Steffi and Martina and it makes me realize that
somehow, I'm not there yet."

Monica's devotion to a new fitness regimen

was not exactly slavish, though. Before the year was out she would make a rare public appearance at a Weight Watcher's party in Monaco; soft and at least a bit overweight, she did not look like a person who had been training with Jackie Joyner-Kersee. In fairness, though, Monica was busy enjoying other aspects of life at the time. She was discovering the world outside of tennis. She would water-ski and jet-ski, often accompanied by close friend Betsy Nagelson, a former professional tennis player and the wife of IMG founder Mark McCormack. She became a voracious reader, with a particular fondness for self-help books. She bought a Fender Stratocaster and tried to mimic the style of her new hero, the late guitar wizard Jimi Hendrix. She spent hours hanging out in bookstores.

In general, she had fun. She gave herself room to grow up. She became a more complete person. Still, there was no denying the emptiness. Monica was, after all, the best female tennis player on the planet. She had been blessed with an extraordinary gift, and it was sad to see that gift gathering dust. There was no timetable, nothing written down. Even her agent, Stephanie Tolleson, had said in February that Monica might not play at all in 1994. In her heart, though, Monica knew: She would be back . . . someday.

"I'm going to play tennis again," she told *Tennis* magazine. "Besides, I don't just want to be remembered for grunting and giggling. I hated being known for that! And I don't just want to be the one who got stabbed. I want to be remembered for my game, and I want to give something back to the game so the players coming up can feel safer on the court—or know that they have a pension plan. There's still a lot I want to accomplish."

On Wednesday, May 17, there was good news out of the Seles camp: Monica and her mother, Esther, had passed their citizenship exams in Miami. "This is a happy day for me," Monica said in a statement released through her publicist. "I am proud to be a United States citizen and very happy my mother and I are now citizens of this great country."

Then, on May 20, just three days before the start of the French Open, Monica began to fight back. First, she announced her desire to have the German Tennis Federation compensate her for the financial losses she had suffered since the attack in Hamburg more than a year earlier. No precise dollar figure was given, but Seles's attorney, Wilhelm Danelzik, indicated his client would seek at least ten million dollars in damages. Seles also formally announced plans to appeal the sentence of her assailant, Gunther Parche.

In a statement released through IMG, Danelzik was critical of security at the Citizen Cup tennis tournament, which was held April 30, 1993, at the Rothenbaum Tennis Center in Hamburg, saying, among other things, that "it can not be

doubted that insufficient security measures"
played a significant role in the attack on Seles.
Moreover, the attorney said, "This year's Citizen
Cup tournament clearly has shown that suffi-
cient security measures to avoid an attack on
players sitting on the benches during breaks
would not only be possible, but reasonable.

"We are not indicating insufficient security at
sporting events in general," Danelzik added.
"There was gross negligence on the part of the
organizers of the Citizen Cup, which resulted in
the attack and serious injury of Miss Seles, and
that attack could have been prevented by adequate security measures."

Monica did not speak with reporters when the
suit was filed. She did, however, release the following statement: "I'm trying very hard to overcome the impact of the stabbing last year. I've
always loved playing tennis, and it's very difficult for me not to be able to live the life I always
thought I would live."

In another statement, Monica's father expressed concern for his daughter's emotional
well-being. "Monica has not been able to
overcome the emotional impact of the knife attack, which continues to be a problem for her,"
Karolj Seles said. "Monica wishes she could have
been playing on the tennis tour by now, but she
is unable to do so. She has been doing her best
to overcome the emotional impact of the stabbing incident. The knife attack on the tennis
court has interrupted her tennis career and her

daily life. Unfortunately Monica is not ready or able to go back to tournament play at this time."

In Seles's absence, Steffi Graf had again come to dominate women's tennis. It was almost as though the game had slipped through a wrinkle in time. Suddenly it was the late 1980s again, and Graf was nothing short of invincible. She had reigned as the game's number-one player for an unprecedented 186 consecutive weeks—from August 17, 1987, to March 10, 1991—and now she reigned again. With Seles out of the picture, Graf had no equal. In the thirteen months since the attack on Seles, Graf had won the French Open, Wimbledon, U.S. Open, and Australian Open—four consecutive Grand Slam events. Her play was impeccable, flawless.

And yet, she hardly seemed like one of the most successful athletes in the world. Indeed, the picture of Steffi Graf that came into focus in 1994 was of a sad and lonely young woman obsessed with the dark side of the human spirit. In a revealing profile that appeared in *Sports Illustrated* in the spring of 1994, Graf admitted to being a perfectionist who found little joy in merely winning. "I'm playing myself out there," she said. "The score is totally meaningless."

Worse, Graf was finding it increasingly difficult to cope with the fishbowl existence of a champion tennis player. She had always been shy, aloof—characteristics that were often mistaken for rudeness. And while maturity, confidence and experience had given her the ability

to fake it for brief periods of time—at press conferences, for example—Graf detested the spotlight. As with Seles, it was purely the joy of the
game that had attracted her to tennis in the first
place. But now there was nothing simple about
the game; about the business; about life.

She was a reluctant superstar, trapped by her
own fame. In Germany she could not step out
her front door without prompting the mobiliza-
tion of an army of paparazzi. And despite her
icy veneer—despite her steadfast refusal to re-
ciprocate the affection of her fans—she was re-
vered. Sometimes their obsession with Graf was
disturbing. The young man who tried to profess
his love by slashing his wrists, for example, or
the fans who regularly trespassed on her property. More and more, Graf was having trouble
accepting and tolerating such behavior. In part,
this stemmed from the attack on Seles. Graf
would later reveal that shortly after hearing of
the assault, her first thought was: *"Oh, God. I
hope it wasn't one of my crazy fans."*

That it was one of her crazy fans came as no
great shock to Graf. It merely served as horrific
confirmation of her worst fears. And if Seles was
clearly the most visible victim in the attack, she
was not the *only* victim. Graf had to live with the
guilt of having played a role, however uninten-
tional. She had to cope with the spectre of
Monica Seles hanging over every point, every
set, every match, every tournament. It was her
penance, to step on the court and hear the

voices—real or imagined:

What if Monica were here?

"It's not easy for me to live with knowing that I'm number one because she was attacked," Graf told *Sports Illustrated*. "I'm playing such good tennis, and I would like to prove it. If Monica were around, I'd have someone to prove it against."

There was no Monica, however. And there was no Jennifer Capriati. Tennis's other bright, young star, who had left the tour after the '93 U.S. Open, citing burnout as the primary reason, was arrested for possession of marijuana in a Miami hotel room in May 1994. It was Capriati's second brush with the law in less than six months; in December she had been charged with shoplifting. Jennifer and Monica—a little more than one year earlier they were considered the future of women's tennis. Now they were gone. And it appeared as though the Grand Slam events were the exclusive domain of Steffi Graf. Even Graf's agent, Phil de Picciotto, had to admit that the game was in a rut.

"This feels like when Tracy Austin and Andrea Jaeger walked away [so young]," he told *Sports Illustrated*. "There's this whole new lost generation—Jennifer, Monica—that should still be playing, and they aren't."

Just as it seemed that Graf would never lose another Grand Slam event, though, her streak came to an end. In the semifinals of the French Open, she was humbled in a straight-set loss to

Mary Pierce, 6–2, 6–2. Pierce then lost to Arantxa Sanchez Vicario in the final.

Although Graf's loss was surprising, it was not a complete shock. Clay, after all, was her weakest surface. Far more startling was her first-round loss to Lori McNeil at Wimbledon. Graf was the three-time defending champion at the All-England Club. She was the number-one seed. She was playing on grass, her favorite surface. None of this seemed to have much of an impact on McNeil, who made Graf the first defending champion in Grand Slam history to be bounced in the first round. The victory was no fluke, either. McNeil was about to have a career tournament. Never before had she advanced beyond the quarterfinal of a Grand Slam event, but at Wimbledon she reached the semifinals. And she very nearly made it to the final. McNeil stretched eventual champion Conchita Martinez to her limit before bowing, 10–8, in the third set.

Martinez went on to capture her first Wimbledon title with an emotional three-set victory over Martina Navratilova, who was seeking her tenth Wimbledon championship. It was a compelling final, primarily because it was Navratilova's last appearance at Wimbledon. When it ended, the crowd stood and cheered mightily. And Martina cried.

At the U.S. Open, Graf arrived in good spirits but nursing a back injury. The ailment did not cause her any great distress, however, until the final. There, Graf routed Sanchez Vicario, 1–6, in the first set, before her back tightened and her game unraveled. Sanchez Vicario wound up with a 1–6, 7–6, 6–4 victory and her first U.S. Open title.

Meanwhile, the former number-one player in the world maintained a low profile. In November Monica made her first public appearance in six months at the Arete Awards for Courage in Sports. She agreed to be a presenter at the Chicago ceremony after hearing the story of one of the honorees: a thirteen-year-old Special Olympian named Sonya Bell who competed in gymnastics, track and field, tennis, and in-line skating. Seles watched videotaped highlights of the girl from Chester, South Carolina, and was moved. Here, thought Monica, is a girl with a real problem, a real disability. Here is a *blind* girl . . . and yet she is fearless.

Here, thought Monica, is a girl I have to meet.

So she flew to Chicago for the show, which was being taped by ESPN for broadcast at a later date. There was no fanfare, no advance notice. She did not speak to the media. She simply participated. Clearly, this one came from the heart. Monica wanted to meet Sonya Bell. She wanted to congratulate the young girl for being so brave, so strong. And the gesture did not go unappreciated. Bell, who received an autographed tennis racquet from Seles, was thrilled to meet one of her heroes.

In the end, it was difficult to say who benefitted most from the encounter.

"We just talked and laughed," Bell told the *Chicago Tribune*. "She laughed the whole time— she was so happy. She was so excited. She needed to get out. It makes me feel good to know I inspired her."

After the Arete Awards, Monica flew to Seattle to meet some friends. On the flight, she could not shake the image of the little blind girl—skating, running, flying through the air . . . *competing!* There was no room for self-pity in that child's life. Why had Monica allowed it to seep into hers?

And then, in Seattle, she experienced another brief encounter that left her shaken. As Monica later related during an interview with *Sports Illustrated*, she passed a homeless man begging on a street corner. Next to him, with a change cup dangling from its mouth, was a sad-eyed dog, shivering in the evening rain. Seles tried to touch the dog, but the animal cowered before her. "His spirit was gone," she said. "And I thought of how my spirit had been broken down." It was, for Monica, another slap in the face, another reminder of how brutal life could be. "I see other people who have no place to go, no family, nobody," she said. "It changed my thought: You don't have it that bad."

You don't have it that bad.

Unfortunately, a variation on that theme was echoed by others who were beginning to lose patience with Monica. Included in that group was her clothing manufacturer, Fila, which filed a lawsuit against Seles in early December for failing to meet her contractual obligation to promote sporting goods for the company. The suit also claimed Seles misled the company by suggesting on three different occasions that she planned to return to the game. Her inactivity, the suit claimed, had cost Fila more than six million dollars.

Seles did not respond publicly to the lawsuit. She left that to her agent, who simply reiterated the company line: There was no timetable for Monica's return; there never had been a timetable; she would resume her tennis career when she felt she was ready.

Chapter 10

JUSTICE DENIED

In the spring of 1995, Monica's resolve seemed to have weakened. Her experience at the Arete Awards, the revelatory moment with the homeless man on the streets of Seattle—neither could sustain her in her darkest moments. Once again, she went into hiding. She worked out on the private courts near her Sarasota mansion.

Some days were good. She would run down every ball, work up a healthy sweat, have a nice meal with her family afterward. She felt safe, secure. Loved.

Other days were not so good. During much of her two-and-a-half-year exile from tennis, Monica was plagued by nightmares. Like a child terrorized by the thought of monsters in the closet, she envisioned Gunther Parche standing in the shadows of her darkened bedroom. She would see his face, his empty eyes, in a dream, and wake up sweating, breathless. And she would hear her own voice. She would hear the screams that filled the Rothenbaum Tennis Club that evening in Hamburg.

"It was eating me alive," she told *Sports Illustrated*. "I'd go out on the court, I could be playing great tennis, and it would all start coming back. I'd say, 'I can't do this.' I pretty much moved to daylight sleeping times. I couldn't sleep at night."

Monica spent most of her time at the Sarasota estate. She had purchased it for her family six months after the stabbing. It was a lavish, opulent place in a development known as Laurel Oak, on the edge of a private country club, with a basketball court and two outdoor tennis courts—one clay, one all-weather. Occasionally, though, she would venture outside the ten-foot, white stucco wall that surrounded the property. More often than not, she traveled alone. Every few weeks someone would report a "Monica sighting" at a local video store or market. And then she would be gone again, back inside the walls. She would be fine for days, even weeks. . . . "Then she's thinking of the stabbing, and she goes to pieces again," her father told *Sports Illustrated*.

In January 1995 Monica tried to take a major step toward recovery. She summoned the strength to look at a videotape of the attack in Hamburg, something she had long declined to do. The theory was this: By confronting the reality of the incident, she could begin to bury it.

If she looked at it, and dealt with it on its own gruesome terms, she might be able to find some sense of closure.

Monica wasn't sure that it would work. But then a group of friends visited over the Christmas holidays, and everyone began discussing the case against Gunther Parche, and suddenly there they all were, gathered around a television set, watching the match in Hamburg. And there was Monica on the screen, sitting in a chair, sipping water from a cup, wiping the sweat off her racquet handle, planning the next game. And then there was a man behind her . . . lunging . . . stabbing. Monica was screaming . . . stumbling . . . falling. People rushed to her side. The man was tackled. All around her there was chaos.

And suddenly Monica was no longer watching the scene on television. She was running out of the room, a hand cupped over her mouth. As the waves of nausea rolled through her body, she suspected that it might still be a long time before she was ready to play tennis, before she was ready to turn her back on a crowd again.

By going back into hiding, Monica fueled renewed speculation about her future. Rumors circulated wildly: She was deeply depressed; she was overweight and unable to play a set of tennis without being exhausted; she was crippled by a fear of failure; she had lost her passion for the game. None of these excuses told the whole story, although there may have been a grain of truth in each of them. At the time, however, Monica was not talking, so no one really knew.

As the date for Gunther Parche's retrial drew near, the media machine picked up steam. Would Monica emerge from her cocoon? Would she testify at the trial? Would she talk about her tennis future? Perhaps in an attempt to answer some of those questions, and to shield his only daughter from further pain, Karolj Seles stepped forward. A man of few words—and most of them delivered in fractured English—Karolj had suffered alongside his daughter since the incident. Moreover, he had endured operations for prostate and stomach cancer in the previous three years.

Through all of the hardship in his life, Karolj Seles maintained a remarkable ability to smile, to laugh. But there is no pain that compares to watching your child suffer. So, in March, Karolj shouldered the burden that was still too heavy for his little girl to carry. He sat down at a typewriter and, in his native tongue, tapped out a letter to the world. It was later translated from Hungarian into English and printed in *The New York Times*, under the following headline: SELES'S LOST TWO YEARS: A FATHER'S LAMENT.

Karolj began with a basic question: When would Monica play tennis again? The answer, of course, was ... *I don't know.* For several paragraphs he replayed the incident in Hamburg in cold, clinical language. It seemed oddly distant, detached, considering his role. Midway through

the article, however, Karolj began to sound like
a father. He spoke passionately about his daughter's love for the game of tennis, about how hard
she had worked, and how free and fulfilled she
felt when she was on the court. Now, he said,
that had been taken from her.

"If you want to achieve something great in
anything, you have to like what you do, work
long and hard and sweat a lot to reach your
goal," Karolj said. "That was Monica. Tennis
was her life.

"An irresponsible man succeeded, with a
knife, in stopping Monica's career, taking the top
ranking away from her. This sport was her love,
her ability, her knowledge. Then, suddenly, she
could not fulfill her ambitions in the game. With
an aching heart, she now sees sorrowfully in the
newspapers, on TV, that the girls continue to
compete and she can't be among them.

"Life and tennis go on, and Monica is slowly
being forgotten. Maybe that's the right thing. It
looks as if everything is O.K., but where is Monica? With that knife in the back, Monica said
farewell to tennis for the time being . . . or is it
forever?"

The cruel and violent interruption of a brilliant
career, however, was not Karolj's primary concern. Like any loving father, he could not bear
to see his daughter's loss of innocence. Never
again would she look at the world in the same
way. Never again would she be so idealistic or
naive. This was inevitable, of course. But it did

not have to happen in such a brutal way.

"Monica lost a lot more than tennis," Karolj wrote. "So far she has lost two beautiful years, two of her best young years, which she can never replace and bring back. Monica was a laughing, cheerful girl. This cheerfulness has disappeared from her face. It's hard for us as parents to see this, but for her it's the hardest."

Karolj then launched into a scathing indictment of the judicial system that had seen fit to release the man who had attacked his daughter. The father was bewildered, frustrated, angry. How, he wondered, could someone wilfully drive a knife blade into the back of another person . . . *and get away with it?* Gunther Parche was a free man; but his daughter, who had never hurt anyone—who would never dream of hurting anyone—was held captive by the memory of the assault. Parche was given a two-year suspended sentence; Monica was given a *life* sentence.

"I trusted that the assailant would answer for his deeds before a German court, that it would bring the appropriate verdict," Karolj wrote. "I was stunned, as I believe that people around the world were stunned, when I learned that the Hamburg court, under the leadership of Judge Elke Bosse, ruled to set the assailant free. This was terrible news to our family. . . . After such a decision, isn't Judge Bosse afraid to look the world in the eye?"

Karolj saw the decision as a miscarriage of justice, as proof that the world really is an unfair place. As any adult knows, it is. But Karolj was an artist, an illustrator sometimes prone to dreamy optimism and sentimentality. Who could fault him for wanting life to be something it wasn't? Especially where his daughter was concerned.

"As Monica's coach, I oversaw her development through defeats as well as victories," he wrote. "Who doesn't lose cannot win, either. I didn't only see to it that Monica should be a perfect sportswoman and that she should see the sport beyond fame and money, but that she be a complete, intelligent lady, one who can find her way in the world when she gets too old for tennis.

"On Tuesday, the Parche case will again be discussed in the Hamburg courts, and I trust that justice will win this time.

"That Monica will return to tennis is only a dream so far, but I hope that in the near future the dream will become a reality. I hope that Monica's dreams will be fulfilled; that she will play professional tennis again."

Karolj Seles was not the only one who wanted to see Monica return to the tennis court. A few days after Karolj's heartfelt story appeared in *The New York Times*, Steffi Graf told reporters that she, too, hoped Seles would soon be playing again. In fact, Graf was even willing to share the number-one ranking with Seles upon her return.

"I have no problem with that," Graf said. "[Monica] definitely needs to get seedings. It would be great for everyone to see her being able to go on the court and to see her play. That would be extraordinary. I hope that will happen."

The WTA, of course, had elected not to freeze Seles's ranking when she left the tour, but now Anne Person Worcester, the WTA's new chief executive officer, suggested that a much more sympathetic stance was likely if she decided to play. Graf, meanwhile, seemed not only excited about the prospect of her rival's comeback, but confident that Seles would regain her previous form. "If you give her time, and if she keeps practicing hard," Graf said, "she will have no problem."

As it had been in October 1993, the prospect of returning to Hamburg was too much for Monica. She could not imagine sitting in a crowded courtroom, sharing her deepest feelings and fears. She could not imagine turning her back on Gunther Parche, which she would have been asked to do. She could not imagine sitting only a few feet away from the man who stabbed her. She could not stand the idea of looking into his eyes—the cold, empty eyes that visited her in her nightmares. *The eyes of a killer.*

So she declined an offer to testify at Parche's second trial, even though she was aware of the potential impact her presence might have. She knew that her reluctance to testify at the first trial had perhaps contributed to Parche's light sen-

tence. Still . . . she could not force herself to go.
She wasn't that strong. Not yet. Instead, she sent
a handwritten letter to appellate Judge Gertraut
Goering, hoping that it would accurately and
strongly convey her sentiments.

"All my life I worked very hard and sacrificed
a lot to be the best tennis player in the world,
and this attack has destroyed all that," Monica
wrote. "This attack has tremendously and irrep-
arably damaged my life, stopped my tennis career.

"I am still suffering the consequences of the
stabbing, and have not been able to overcome
the effects of the stabbing, although I continue
my medical counseling. I only want proper justice. I was a nineteen-year-old girl when he
stabbed me. He has not been successful in his
attempt to kill me, but he has destroyed my life."

In explaining her decision not to testify, Monica wrote, "I was not going to turn my back on
this criminal again. I am still haunted by the
memory of seeing him behind me as he attempted to stab me a second time in 1993. Why
should I have to see him again just to try to see
that justice is done?"

In the seventeen months since his first trial,
Gunther Parche had conducted a reasonably successful public relations campaign on his own behalf. He had offered a public apology to Seles.
He granted access to the media, and always
painted himself as a sad man who had been sub-

jected to a terrible, lonely childhood. He was not
a dangerous criminal; he was merely a pathetic
loner.

Testimony at the second trial, however, revealed a darker side of Parche. Yes, he was obsessed with Steffi Graf—his room at his aunt's
house was nothing less than a shrine to Graf, in
fact, with posters and photographs on the walls
and a video library of her tournaments next to
the television. He wrote anonymous letters to
Graf on numerous occasions and once sent her
money in the hope that she would use it to buy
a piece of jewelry—sort of a present from her
secret admirer. Indeed, Parche made no effort to
hide his affection for Graf. As he said at the retrial, "She is a dream creature whose eyes spar-
kle like diamonds and whose hair shines like
silk. I would walk through fire for her."

Was Parche merely deluded, though? Alleg-
edly, he had stabbed Seles in twisted attempt to
cripple her, to make sure she would be unable
to play and thus be forced to relinquish her grip
on the number-one ranking. Graf would then be
where she belonged—in Parche's eyes, at least:
at the top of the ladder. Evidence at the trial,
though, indicated that perhaps a deeper, uglier
motive for the attack existed, a racial motive.
Parche testified that he believed "Serbs today are
the worst and most serious danger in Europe."
He also said he "wanted to teach the parents of
the Serb [Seles] a lesson."

As Monica herself later pointed out, "His

words in court were, I hate her, I hate the Serbs. He said that had I been a German or an American, he would not have stabbed me."

German political and legal analysts also suggested that Parche's light sentence might have been connected to a racial issue. Seles was not a Serb. She was an ethnic Hungarian who had grown up in an area of Yugoslavia now controlled by Serbs. Truth mattered less than perception, though. Germany had backed Croatia during World War II, and now the Croats were fighting the Serbs. Lines were being drawn. Perhaps the freeing of Gunther Parche was a symbol of support.

Perhaps not.

To Monica, it really didn't matter. She wanted justice. She wanted to know that it *wasn't* acceptable to attack another human being. She wanted Gunther Parche put behind bars.

Instead, Judge Goring upheld Parche's suspended sentence, saying it was justified in light of his confession, apology, lack of prior arrests, and diminished mental capacity. "Our law does not function on the principle, 'an eye for an eye,'" Goring said. The judge added that it seemed unlikely Parche intended to kill Seles, given the type of wound he inflicted. "We can't rule out that he meant to do more than he did to Miss Seles, but we also can't prove this," Goring said.

Seles's lawyer, Gerhardt Strate, had sought a five-year prison sentence (Hamburg prosecutors asked for a thirty-three-month sentence), and was obviously unhappy with the decision, but noted that without Seles's testimony, the case against Parche was weak. It depended almost entirely on eyewitness accounts. "Their testimony had to be clear and consistent, and it wasn't," Strate told *Tennis Week* magazine. "There were contradictions. We had to explain the physical wound, why it was only a mark on her back. The guard placed behind Monica said that when he saw Parche attack, he grabbed him by the trousers and [minimized] the motion of the stabbing. Other witnesses stated that they held his arm behind his back so he could not stab her again. A doctor testified that the wound was not as severe as it could have been because the skin on the back is so thick. But I believe he had no control of where he would stab her and he could have killed her."

Sports psychologist Jerry Russel May testified that Seles was still suffering from post-traumatic stress syndrome. Like war veterans and other victims of violent crime, she was experiencing emotional problems related to the attack. "She is fearful, cries, and feels very nervous," May testified. "She is not sleeping well and has nightmares. She's frightened that Mr. Parche could attack her again."

One court-appointed psychiatrist described Parche as "a perverse, scurrilous loner who would never have been noticed if the problem with Steffi Graf had not emerged." Aside from that fixation, however, the psychiatrist said Parche was essentially harmless. A second court-appointed psychiatrist echoed that sentiment. "The evaluations," Judge Goring noted, "were both positive."

In the sports world the verdict was met with a predictable mix of anger, awe, and disgust. The president of the German Tennis Association, Clause Stauder, told *The New York Times* that he wanted "a verdict that would have a deterrent effect." Oliver Moller, a German soccer player who was stabbed in 1994, was similarly disappointed, saying, "Something like this must be far more severely punished."

The WTA's Anne Person Worcester agreed. "It defies logic that a person can commit a premeditated assault witnessed by millions of people around the world without being sentenced to jail time," she said. "The WTA tour firmly believes that the court has perpetuated the injustice in this case and that the defendant should have been sentenced to significant prison time."

Like most observers, Worcester was speaking from her heart. She could not fathom the court's decision. Parche had stabbed this young woman in front of seven thousand witnesses. It was violent. It was malicious. It was deliberate. What more proof was needed?

Donna Doherty, editor of *Tennis* magazine, vented in similar fashion: "With the latest verdict in the retrial of Seles's assailant, Gunther Parche, I can only express dismay once again about another miscarriage of justice in this never-ending saga. I have tried to be objective and nonethnocentric, trying to understand how some cultures cane people's bare bottoms for spray-painting graffiti, and some cultures still hang people for treason, while other cultures allow a crazed man wielding a knife to plunge it into someone's back and walk away without so much as a slap on the wrist."

In actuality, Parche's sentence was consistent with German precepts. There was insufficient evidence to convict him of attempted murder, and "grievous bodily harm" was a far less significant charge. Parche had no prior convictions of any kind. His record was spotless. Those facts, combined with the psychiatrists' testimony and Seles's refusal to appear at the trial, made it difficult for the judge to impose a harsher sentence. In a U.S. court of law Parche might have been ordered confined to a mental institution for a period of time, but that is far less common in Germany.

So he walked.

Meanwhile, a few days before the second trial ended, Monica traveled to Williamsburg, Virginia, to attend the dedication of the McCormack-Nagelsen Tennis Center at William & Mary College. She made the trip as a favor to a pair of friends: IMG founder Mark McCormack and his wife, Betsy Nagelsen. It was an important step in Monica's recovery, for she had not made a public appearance since the Arete

Awards. A few weeks earlier she had met with McCormack to discuss her future. McCormack was compassionate and supportive. But he also had a business to run, and now he needed to know: *When, Monica? When?*

"I went to a meeting with Mark, and he was asking me questions like, 'What do you see in your future?' " Seles told *People* magazine. "And I said, 'Well, I love to play tennis. That's what I wanted to do all my life.' He said, 'Why don't you try it again?' And I said, 'Okay.' "

They sketched out a blueprint for her return, including security precautions, training schedules, endorsement opportunities, and medical support. By the time she arrived in Williamsburg, the wheels had been set in motion, though almost no one knew it at the time.

To the casual observer, Monica seemed to have recaptured much of her old enthusiasm that weekend. There were banquets and dances on Friday and Saturday nights. There were people to meet, hands to shake. She smiled and laughed the way she always had. In sum, she was her old charming self. On Sunday morning Monica surprised a small group of spectators when she walked onto a tennis court and rallied with one of the school's administrators. It wasn't a tournament. It wasn't even a practice session. But it was an important moment, nonetheless: For the first time since the stabbing, Monica hit a ball in public.

There was no explanation given. Presumably,

she felt comfortable in that setting. And, perhaps, she was confident that justice was being served in a courtroom in Germany. The end was near. Soon, she could get on with her life.

But then it was Monday morning, and Monica was stuck in an airport in Atlanta, waiting to change planes during her trip back to Sarasota. She was curious about the trial, so she called her agent. The news came through the telephone like a bolt of electricity. Gunther Parche was a free man again. Monica turned to her mother for comfort and began to cry.

For the record, Seles, through her agent, offered only this statement on the day the second trial ended: "I am as surprised as everyone else, and I just don't understand this."

The following week, during a telephone interview with *Sports Illustrated*, Monica expressed a combination of anger and bewilderment: "How can anyone say that it's O.K. to do what this man did to another human being? How can they say it's O.K.? I'm a human being."

She also defended her decision not to appear at the trial. "How can they have expected me to go back there and testify?" Monica said. "When I heard I would have to sit in the courtroom with my back to him, I knew it was the one hundred percent absolute right decision. I mean, the man stabbed me.

"There was the way he did it, the idea that he put the knife in my back, pulled it out, and was going to do it again. I can still see the hate in his face that I saw when I turned around. And they say he doesn't have to go to jail at all? I don't understand. I'm just . . . so . . . . confused."

In a separate interview with *USA Today*, Monica reiterated her fear of Parche. But, for the first time, she publicly expressed hope that she could put the incident behind her. If Gunther Parche was truly a monster, then perhaps it was time to fight back. "In my mind I see his face," she said. "I see a lot of hatred. When he did this, I looked back, and this guy was holding him. A lot of nights when I wake up, I think he's right there where I am sleeping. Now I don't trust, I just don't trust. But then again, you can't let someone take away your life. I can't let anybody do that."

A second appeal was filed in Hamburg's highest court, but Seles's lawyer was quick to dash any hope of a different outcome; since no new testimony would be allowed, the appeal would hinge on contesting and interpreting various points of law. "I can only say that the Seles [family] definitely wants to appeal this verdict again," Gerhardt Strate told *Tennis Week*. "There should be some grounds for appeal, but it will be difficult. Generally, in appeals, judges favor the defense. I hope we can change it, but it will be difficult."

In the wake of the disturbing outcome of the retrial, speculation about Monica's career heightened. Clearly she had been preparing for a comeback. There was talk of an appearance in the Federation Cup, or perhaps in World TeamTennis. But now, with Parche free, all bets were off. Billie Jean King, the Federation Cup captain, had spoken with Seles on several occasions in the previous few months. It was her opinion that Monica would probably retreat once again. "I don't think [she'll come back soon]," King told the *Tampa Tribune*. "With that decision, I think she's the same as before."

Perhaps not, though. Monica continued to practice. She continued to play tennis, albeit privately. And when she played, she played well. "She's absolutely belting the ball so hard and so deep," said McCormack, who sometimes played doubles with Seles. "She's certainly good enough to be number two or number three in the world immediately."

McCormack had more than a casual interest in Monica's career, of course, and a skeptic might have accused him of being hyperbolic for the sake of publicity. Word of these private sessions was leaking out, though, and virtually everyone who saw Monica play agreed that she had lost almost nothing during her absence. Physically, she was ready to play. Emotionally, though? That was another matter.

In an effort to encourage Monica, Anne Person Worcester extended an olive branch on behalf of the WTA, which had not been quite as supportive as it might have been during her absence. In addition to dealing with the trauma of the attack and the release of Gunther Parche, Monica was still smarting from the WTA's decision not to freeze her ranking two years earlier. Worcester made no specific promises about what would happen if Monica decided to resume her playing career, but her public stance was conciliatory.

"Monica is one of the most intriguing figures in sports," Worcester told *Tennis Week* in April 1995. "She transcends women's tennis. Everyone is interested in what happens to Monica. Great matches at Lipton were overshadowed by articles on Monica and the trial. It would be great to have Monica back because she obviously attracts interest amongst a general market.

"There is a whole new leadership now in the game and we have made it clear that Monica will be given special consideration. But until she indicates she will return, any other discussion is premature."

If the verbiage was deliberately vague, the message still came through loud and clear: Monica Seles would not be thrown back into the pile like any other player coming back from a two-year layoff. No one expected her to play in qualifiers or invest a year in achieving a respectable computer ranking. She was unique. She was the game's premier player. On and off the court, she was a star, and when she was not playing, it affected everyone associated with the sport of tennis. So the rules would be bent; if necessary, the rules would be rewritten. The WTA wanted Monica back, and it would take whatever steps were necessary.

Even her fellow players were vocal in their support. Monica had not always been the most popular player on the women's tour, in part because of her phenomenal success, and in part because she kept to herself. She had a very small entourage, and virtually everyone in it was named Seles. "It wasn't like she was rude or anything," said Darrell Fry, a writer for the *St. Petersburg Times* who has covered Seles for nearly a decade. "She just didn't make much of an effort. She was always with her family."

The resentment that periodically leaked out of the locker room and into post-match press conferences was fading. At the very least, it was being repressed. Each week, it seemed, a new player was stepping forward to offer words of encouragement and support for Monica. Included in that group was Gabriela Sabatini. "We need Monica," Sabatini said. "We'd like to have her back. I hope she does what makes her happy, whether that means playing or not. But now the questions we are always being asked are about her."

Conchita Martinez was similarly supportive, despite the fact that she would be directly affected if Monica were immediately given a high ranking. More and more, it seemed, that scenario was likely. By late spring, the general assumption was that when Monica returned, she would be given co–number one status with Steffi Graf. That meant Martinez would drop from number three to number four. "It's a hard decision and I don't know what's going to happen," Martinez told *Tennis* magazine. "I feel good about helping her. Monica was number one, so why not put her at number one?"

Added Chris Evert: "Sounds great to me. She deserves that. She was number one, and what happened to her happened at a tournament."

If the majority of players were supportive of Monica, a few remained mildly annoyed. Empathy was the politically correct emotion to display, and usually that is what the public saw. Beneath the surface, though, impatience bubbled.

"I just don't understand why nobody can talk to her, why we're left guessing all the time," Jana Novotna told *Tennis*. "And I don't understand this, either: If she's so special and tough and loves the game so much, how come she has disappeared? Doesn't she really miss it?"

While it was tempting to chastise Novotna for an apparent lack of compassion, it was also hard not to admire her candor. Monica *was* supposed to be one of the toughest players in the game. Her success was less a byproduct of natural talent than an indomitable spirit. So . . . where was that spirit now? Where was the mental toughness that had made her the youngest number-one player in history?

Yes, Monica had suffered terribly. She had been the victim of a brutal and unforgivable attack. But she had survived. She had recovered. Wasn't it time to get on with life?

"These kinds of tragedies—rape, assault, accidents—happen, and they knock people off the horse," Pam Shriver said. "You've got to be able to get back up on the horse, and Monica hasn't. She has a life, but it's not *the* life. The question is: What's so different about her?"

The answer, of course, was . . . *everything*. Monica was not a typical tennis prodigy, plucked from the family nest before she was old enough to change her own clothes and sentenced to adolescence in some secluded sports gulag. She had a strong family support system. She was taught by her father. She was as much artist as athlete. If she had the will of a champion, she also had the soul of a poet, and that combination often tormented her.

Ironically, the love and support Monica received from her family may actually have obstructed her recovery. Victims of post-traumatic stress syndrome must deal with this unfortunate reality: The world is often a harsh and unkind place. Rather than face that reality, Monica had retreated to the sanctuary of home and hearth. And while the warmth of her family was a soothing balm, in the long run it may have compounded the damage to her psyche. In a story that appeared in the August 1995 issue of *Tennis*, in which Seles's prolonged period of recovery was intensely analyzed, psychologist Jim Loehr offered this explanation.

"Because tennis parents usually recognize that they're putting their kids under extraordinary stress, they try to protect them from other pressures, to buffer them from the real world. The result, though, can be like a cast on a broken bone: The muscles begin to atrophy. So many young tennis players end up being vulnerable in a broader sense. Monica only knew tennis. The assault was, for her, an absolutely earth-shattering confrontation with the ugly side of life. She trusted the world around her—the world her parents had constructed for her—only to have it destroyed, and at her most golden time."

Added Chris Evert sympathetically, the fear can be even worse "if you feel your parents' own fear, as maybe Monica does. I know from my own kids that if they think *I'm* afraid of something, they'll back off from it right away. Maybe what Monica needs is a slumber party with some of us players."

Norman Tamarkin, a Washington, D.C. psychiatrist, suggested that perhaps the stabbing had extinguished Seles's competitive fire. Tennis, he said, is "symbolic aggression, a way of channeling aggression. The stabbing may have destroyed the boundaries between real aggression and tennis aggression, and she may now feel that she can't be as tough on court. If that [killer] instinct gets short-circuited, consciously or unconsciously, it could have a serious impact on whether the person feels confident about playing again."

More than one observer wondered whether

Monica had the necessary motivation to begin playing again. After all, she had already accomplished so much. And it wasn't like she needed the money. She had a close circle of friends and loved ones with whom she could share her life. Unless she truly missed the game—missed the competition and the roar of the crowd when she crunched a backhand winner—then there was no reason to play.

Those closest to her, however, suspected that Monica *did* miss those things. And they knew it was only a matter of time before the urge to play became overwhelming, and pushed aside the fear. When that happened she would step outside the walls of her estate, pick up a racquet . . . and play. But what type of player would she be?

"At first, you might see lapses in her concentration," U.S. Davis Cup captain Tom Gullikson told *Tennis*. "And perhaps in her great instinct for putting matches away. But the only way to get match tough is to play matches."

As for a timetable, well, it was hard to say. Certainly it would be ridiculous to expect the Monica Seles of 1995 to play like the Monica Seles of 1993. In Gullikson's opinion, Seles would have no trouble traversing the long road back. But it would take time, he said. "At least a year."

Considering all she had endured, that seemed a reasonable estimate. Jim Loehr went one step further, though. He suggested Seles forget about rankings and prize money and titles altogether. "My advice," he said, "would be this: Try to

reignite the love affair you had with tennis; try
to regain the passion and fun you found there
before."

Nick Bollettieri, Monica's former coach, also
offered words of support and encouragement. In
a column that appeared in the June 22 issue of
Tennis Week magazine, Bollettieri not only attempted to bury the hatchet with his estranged
pupil, but praised her unconditionally.

"I haven't spoken with Monica for several
years except to say hello at the U.S. Open in
1994," Bollettieri wrote. "What I can say without
hesitation, however, based on almost five years
of working with Monica, is that no other student
of mine (and there have been thousands) had the
determination, concentration, and drive that
Monica possessed.

"The women's game has improved tremendously in the past five years, but it is hard to say
for sure if there is another player out there with
Monica's strong mental game and iron will.
Therefore, I unequivocally will go on record to
say that if Monica decides to return to the game,
she could certainly assume her rightful position
among the top three players in the world.

"Just recently, Steffi Graf said it better than
anyone when she said that with the absence of
Monica, she finds it difficult to compete at her
level and maintain her interest in the game. In
short, the game needs Monica. . . . I would make
the assumption that if she is anywhere as mentally tough as she was, a return to the game and

all the hype and attention it would generate at a fever pitch wouldn't touch her. Monica is the Michael Jordan of tennis. She falls into a category few athletes can fill."

Chapter 11

TENNIS, ANYONE?

When Chris Evert arrived at her gate at Miami International Airport in late May, she was surprised to see Monica Seles. But not nearly as surprised as Seles was to see her. Monica was on her way to Paris for a series of meetings with WTA officials. The subject of those meetings: her computer ranking.

Monica was trying to slip out of town quietly, and the last thing she wanted was an impromptu meeting with Evert, who now wore several professional hats. Not only was she a former player, endorser, and tennis ambassador—she also was a broadcaster covering the French Open for NBC. In other words, she was a reporter. And reporters like to ask questions and then reveal the answers to the entire world. That, after all, is their job. So, when Seles spotted Evert, she fairly froze.

"I did a double take," Evert told *Sports Illus-*

trated. "She was with an IMG agent, and as soon as they saw me, the agent covered her up. I went up and said, 'Monica, I can't pretend I don't see you. I just want to say hi.' " Seles retreated to the back of the plane. Afterward, at the baggage carousel, Evert ran into her again. "I hope to see you back soon," she said.

In fact, that was the plan. Monica had been working out regularly at her home. In April she had been visited by Martina Navratilova, who was in Florida for a Federation Cup match. The two talked, as they had on several previous occasions. This time, though, the tennis gear came out. They hit casually, lightly, but Navratilova could see right away that Monica was still Monica. All she needed was a little time and encouragement. Maybe, Navratilova thought, she needs a friend.

Monica did not make it to Stade Roland Garros, but she managed to steal the show at the French Open anyway. Midway through the tournament, in the first week of June, she announced that her twenty-seven-month sabbatical was about to end. Her comeback would begin with an exhibition match in Atlantic City, New Jersey, on July 29. Her opponent would be none other than Martina Navratilova.

Well, that was all anyone in Paris needed to hear. Suddenly the French Open became little more than a backdrop for the biggest tennis story of the year: the return of Monica Seles. This, of

course, was unfair to the women who competed—particularly Steffi Graf and Arantxa Sanchez Vicario, each of whom had spent time at
the top of the computer rankings in the previous
year.

In the French Open final, Graf defeated Sanchez Vicario, 7–5, 4–6, 6–0, to recapture the number-one spot. It was a marvelous performance,
especially in light of the fact that Graf's chronically bad back had been bothering her, and she
wasn't even sure she would be physically capable of playing in Paris. Moreover, clay was her
least favorite surface, so there was no reason to
believe she would march so emphatically to another Grand Slam title. She deserved praise and
admiration.

Afterward, though, no one really wanted to
talk to Graf about her match against Sanchez Vicario.

They wanted to talk about Monica.

Fortunately, Graf was more than willing to indulge their curiosity, in part because she, too,
was excited by the prospect of seeing Seles with
a racquet in her hand.

"I love challenges," she said. "The most fun
you get is when you have tough matches and
you're pushed to your limits. Monica was one of
the players who did that to me. So ... I've
missed her."

Too, there was the matter of guilt. No one
held Graf accountable for the actions of Gunther
Parche, and no one expected her to shoulder the

blame for Seles's absence. Still, it was always there, always in the back of her mind. Like Monica, she lived with the memory of the attack; she lived with the consequences. Because she so rarely displayed any emotion, some observers felt Graf had buried the incident. But she hadn't.

"I don't think any human can do that who has any heart," Graf said after her French Open victory. "All these tournaments—it was really hard for me because I didn't know what was happening. I got questions constantly, and I felt . . . he said he was my fan, so it's impossible not to feel guilty. If something like that happens, you cannot put it behind you."

In a demonstration of support, Graf reiterated in Paris her belief that Seles should be given special consideration by the WTA. The WTA Players' Association had been toying with the idea of suggesting Seles share the number-three spot upon her return. In that way, she would supplant neither Graf nor Sanchez Vicario. Graf, though, felt a bit more generosity was in order.

"When she left she was number one," Graf said. "And it's going to be hard enough for her to come back anyway. We should do anything possible for her."

Graf wasn't alone in that sentiment. Nick Bollettieri, who had helped Monica's recovery by occasionally supplying practice partners from his tennis academy, publicly aligned himself with the Seles camp, despite their tumultuous history.

"There has been much discussion concerning the WTA's treatment of Monica's ranking," Bollettieri wrote in *Tennis Week*. "With respect to this, my thirty-eight-year career in the tennis industry has taught me that it is virtually impossible to forecast the decisions which the WTA may make. As a result, I have tried to steer away from bureaucracy and the various establishments, assuming a personal creed to take care of myself, my family, my students, and the Academy, and let others worry about themselves.

"If I had been on the WTA board, however, my vote could have been cast in favor of freezing her ranking. This tragedy was far more serious than any illness or injury for which the rule was designed. Monica Seles was the WTA Tour's marquee player. It made no stand on her behalf, and sadly, no exception. This was a tremendous error. Rules, as they say, are made to be broken, or at the very least, adjusted."

Coming as it did from a man whose livelihood depended nearly as much on diplomacy as it did coaching ability, this was a statement with some muscle. Bollettieri and Seles had endured a bitter breakup, and yet, here he was, chastising the WTA for treating her unfairly. If anyone had an axe to grind with Monica, it was Bollettieri. And yet, he could only sympathize with her. Whatever the reasons behind their estrangement, they were meaningless in light of what Monica had been through in the previous two years. It was time to set aside personal grudges. It was time to cut through the red tape.

It was time for Monica Seles to play tennis.

Steffi Graf won her sixth Wimbledon title on July
9. In a mesmerizing display of skill and courage,
she overcame a bone spur in her back to defeat
Sanchez Vicario, 4–6, 6–1, 7–5. Their final—a rematch of the French Open championship—was
nothing short of sensational. Graf and Sanchez
Vicario fought brilliantly, defiantly. It was a fit-
ting conclusion to a memorable Wimbledon—
number one meeting number two in an epic
match on Centre Court. The third set included a
thirty-two-point game in which the players
reached deuce thirteen times. Like Ping-Pong,
grass-court tennis is notoriously quick, with rallies often lasting only a few shots. This game was
a wonder, though, stretching more than twenty
minutes as the crowd sat spellbound.

Graf eventually broke Sanchez Vicario to take
a 6–5 lead and then held serve to end the match.
It was her thirty-second consecutive victory in
1995—without a defeat—and when it was over,
she could not conceal her joy. She ran into the
stands to share a joyful embrace with her family,
and then sprinted briefly out of sight before
shouting triumphantly. A few minutes later she
proudly hoisted the champion's trophy and
soaked up the applause. This was Graf's moment, perhaps the finest moment of her career.

Within two hours, though, she was upstaged
again. On the other side of the Atlantic, at the

Special Olympics World Summer Games in New Haven, Connecticut, Monica Seles ended her self-imposed exile.

She had accepted an invitation to present medals to the winners of the tennis competition, and she handled that task with typical style and charm. Escorted by Eunice Shriver, the founder of the Games, Monica received a warm greeting from the crowd. Then, with about five hundred people watching, she and her father conducted a clinic for the athletes.

They were, of course, a huge hit.

Afterward, Monica held her first major press conference in nearly two years. She appeared to be slightly nervous, and though she giggled nervously and spoke in a dialect all her own—just as she had before the stabbing—there was no denying that her innocence had been lost.

While Monica was clearly upbeat and excited, an air of suspicion and fear permeated the affair. Reporters covering the event were required to present two forms of identification: the usual Special Olympics press credential, along with a wrist band issued to reporters covering Seles's clinic and press conference. Organizers of the Special Olympics made it quite clear that the additional security measures were dictated by the Seles camp.

When it came time to meet the press, Monica admitted to suffering from a pretty severe case of the jitters. Even in this relatively peaceful, supportive environment, she said, it was difficult to be surrounded by strangers, to hear the applause, to feel the heat of the crowd.

"I was nervous," she said of the clinic. "But in ten to fifteen minutes, I was comfortable and back to myself."

There was little mystery surrounding the press conference. Monica was expected to officially announce her intention to resume her playing career, and that is precisely what she did. The only question was . . . when? The exhibition match against Navratilova was set, but what about *real* tennis?

"I feel ready to play, physically and emotionally," she said. "And for me to go another step, I need to do this, and I need to go back to something I love to do. I hope to play the U.S. Open. I plan to play. I plan to be there. I believe I can do it. But I'm not entered in it yet. I would like to play something beforehand."

If the purpose of the press conference was to formally announce Monica's comeback, it became something more. It became an opportunity for her to address many of the questions that had surfaced in the media during her prolonged absence. Monica had granted only a handful of interviews, and now she sat before a group of reporters, all of whom wanted to know intimate details of her recovery. Painful as it was to bare her soul once again—to replay in her mind the events of April 30, 1993—Monica understood her responsibility. This was her coming-out party, timed for maximum exposure (the day of the

Wimbledon final) and minimum annoyance (an
ocean away from Wimbledon and its attendant
media horde). If she really wanted people to believe the emotional scars were healing, if she
wanted them to believe she was serious about
playing tennis again, then she had to answer the
questions. All of them.

Interestingly, she never uttered the word
"stabbing." She danced all around it, made ref-
erence to it. But she never let it pass her lips.
"Emotionally, it was very real to me," Monica
said. "I worked hard to overcome it. It took a
long time. But it did happen. Somebody coming
up and doing that to you . . .

"I always felt safest on the tennis court. That
was taken away from me."

Contrary to some published reports, Monica
insisted that she never really considered retirement. Always, in the back of her mind, she knew
she would be back. She simply didn't know
when. "I had good days and bad days," she said.
"Now it is time to move on and forget what happened. It's time to have fun and play great tennis."

Skeptics, naturally, questioned the timing of
the announcement. It was, they said, further evidence that Monica was not merely a flake with
a gift for playing tennis, but a shrewd and savvy
businesswoman who knew how to use the media
to her own advantage. These were the same people who cynically questioned the severity of
Monica's scars—emotional and physical—the

ones who accused her of holding out for a big
insurance payment, and of trying to wriggle out
of her contract with Fila.

To which Monica replied . . . *nonsense!*

"Some people felt, Monica is faking it, but
why would I fake it?" she told *Sports Illustrated.*
"There's no logic. I love to play tennis, and for
the past two-and-a-half years, I have lost all my
income. I've not received anything from the endorsements, and I've never had an insurance
policy. Someone said, 'Monica orchestrated this.'
Why wouldn't I play? It doesn't make sense."

These and other myths and half-truths she attempted to dispel in New Haven. In the end,
though, all she could do was smile and throw
up her hands. Proof would come when she
stepped on a court. But even there, she asked for
patience. She had been practicing hard, and she
was confident in her ability to be competitive on
the women's tour—right away. But as far as
playing the way she had played in 1993, before
the stabbing . . . well, that was an unreasonable
request. "I have been away two-and-a-half
years," Monica said. "I will need time to get
used to the matches and the setting."

At Wimbledon the WTA temporarily backed
away from its proposal to grant Monica a co-
number-one ranking with Graf. Some members
of the players association grew skittish about any
sort of long-term commitment (which would
have left Seles with a number-one ranking for as
many as twelve tournaments, regardless of her

performance in those tournaments), and eventually the issue was tabled. At the time of her appearance in New Haven, Monica was still a Woman Without a Ranking.

"They agree they want Monica back," Martina Navratilova said. "But they're all defending their own little turf."

Not that Monica seemed to care in the least.

"I never asked for any ranking," she said. "I made it clear all I wanted to do is play. I just want to go back and have some fun. If I'm good, I'll be there. If I'm not, then I don't deserve to be there."

On Tuesday, July 11, Seles's lawyer, Gerhardt Strate, announced a second appeal against Parche's two-year suspended sentence. According to Strate, Parche should not have been charged with "causing grievous bodily harm," but rather with attempted manslaughter. And he should have been sentenced accordingly. It was a bold and aggressive step on the part of the Seles camp, in light of the fact that the prosecution had decided to drop its appeal.

"We decided not to proceed with the appeal," prosecutor Ruediger Bagger told the Associated Press, "because we concluded that we could not get a different sentence."

Perhaps it was a waste of time on Seles's part to chase justice. But she did it anyway. Regardless of the outcome of the appeal, she could take solace in the knowledge that she had exhausted all options. She had fought back, and there was dignity in that.

On July 19, word leaked out that the WTA and the members of its players association had finally come to an agreement on the issue of Seles's ranking. A formal announcement would not come until the following day, but it was apparent that Seles would be offered a co–number one ranking.

Monica was delighted to hear the news but tried to downplay any lingering controversy. "There was a written proposal of a ranking and then it was taken back," she told the *Associated Press*. "I didn't understand that. I'm happy about it, of course, but I was going to play either way."

Navratilova, the president of the WTA Players Association, and the player who had been most supportive of Monica, said the WTA's waffling on the matter could be attributed to a lack of communication. There was no animosity, she said. "The bottom line is, the players want Monica back and perhaps they didn't understand the ranking system and how it works."

The agreement called for Seles and Graf to share the number-one ranking for the first six tournaments in which Seles played. "The players had no problem with that," Navratilova said. "The only fair way for her to come back is number one, because that's how she left. There was no discussion about that. The discussion was about how long she would keep it."

A resolution to that problem was announced
the next day, when the WTA formally introduced Seles as its co–number one, along with
Steffi Graf. They would share the top spot for six
tournaments or twelve months from the date
Monica played her first WTA event—whichever
came first. After that, Seles would be co-ranked
based upon her ranking average, which would
be determined by using a reduced minimum di-
visor through her first fourteen tournaments—or
through her first eighteen months of competition. After that, a traditional formula would be
used to determine her computer ranking.

"Monica's return has been a much-discussed
subject for more than two years," said the WTA's
Anne Person Worcester. "Recently there has
been a great deal of confusion about the actual
plan the tour was proposing. We are delighted
to report that all the tour's constituencies—the
players, tournament, and ITF [International Tennis Federation]—jointly support the co–number
one ranking for Monica's return to the tour."

Worcester was understandably relieved to
have the issue resolved, and to have the game's
premier player back in uniform. But she wasn't
the only one smiling. Navratilova was equally
pleased, for she had been at the center of the
ranking maelstrom. As president of the players
association, she was obligated to defend the con-
cerns of her fellow players; as a close friend of
Monica's, however, she felt another type of responsibility. Reconciling those conflicting duties

was not easy, but Navratilova, as impressive and thoughtful a champion as the sport of tennis has ever known, was the perfect woman for the job.

"Monica was the victim of an unprecedented crime in sports, and we wanted to acknowledge her number-one ranking before she was stabbed and forced to leave the WTA tour more than two years ago," Navratilova said. "Monica never asked for special ranking consideration, but she has accepted the tour's plan and has indicated that she will be returning to the tour and playing in the U.S. Open."

Indeed, Seles had by then filed an official application for entry into the U.S. Open. She would play in New York, but not before tuning up with a smaller tournament, and not before meeting Navratilova—her friend and surrogate big sister—in an exhibition in Atlantic City.

"Without Martina this would never have gone through," Monica said. "She's the one who started it."

As much as Navratilova liked Seles, her motives weren't entirely altruistic. She was smart enough, and experienced enough, to know that tennis desperately needed Monica. The game had been in something of a slump ever since her departure. When Monica returned—with her goofy giggle and her exuberant grunt, not to mention her awesome talent—interest in the game would be rekindled. With Monica came sponsors and endorsements and media exposure . . . and fans.

Maturity and experience had given Navratilova a broader perspective than some of her fellow players. She saw the big picture: Monica was an enormous draw, and for anyone to let petty jealousy or territoriality stand in the way of her return was absolutely foolish.

"No matter how great a sport is, it needs stars," Navratilova told the Associated Press. "Michael Jordan was sorely missed in the NBA. The league got a boost when he came back. It's the same with women's tennis. When Monica was stabbed, we lost our number one. To have her back will be a great boost."

Exhibition matches are usually disposable affairs. Ignored by all but the most ardent fans and forgotten by everyone upon their conclusion, exhibitions are the junk food of professional tennis: tasty but utterly lacking in substance. Players accept large appearance fees to stage a public workout. They smile a lot, sign a few autographs, and try not to get hurt. Typically, the outcome is not important.

There was, however, nothing typical about the July 29 match between Seles and Navratilova at the Atlantic City Convention Center. That much was evident in the days leading up to the event, which garnered the type of media coverage usually reserved for Grand Slam tournaments.

On Thursday, July 27, television cameras were brought to the Laurel Oak Country Club in Sarasota so that Monica could conduct a press conference via satellite. It was time to hype the comeback, even though it really needed no hyping. As she had in New Haven, Monica endured a round of questions about her physical and emotional health. She was asked to step back in time and recount the details of the stabbing and the post-traumatic stress that kept her out of tennis for two and a half years.

To her credit, Monica fielded the questions flawlessly, which was further proof that she really was ready to mount a comeback. She was prepared for the glare of the spotlight that would surely accompany her every move—at least for a while.

"Once in a while some memories still come back," she said of the attack. "Emotionally it's been very weird. Suddenly I was playing great tennis and I felt very good at being number one. The next morning I woke up and it all changed. I don't think that anything good has come of it."

There was no way of knowing what to expect from Monica when she stepped on the court Saturday night. She was an inch taller and about fifteen to twenty pounds heavier than when she last played a match. She had grown up. She was stronger. But she was not nearly in peak condition, and certainly she expected her game to be more than a bit creaky. Rust was inevitable. None of that mattered, though. The important thing was that she was determined to play. She would hear the crowd cheering, and she would draw on that energy as she threw her entire body into a two-fisted backhand . . . or forehand.

After twenty-seven months, she would be home.

"I'm just going to play great tennis and have fun," Monica said. "I've promised myself to just enjoy it, to feel the excitement and just play. In the last two and a half years I've not had so many fun days."

That she would be nervous was a given; Monica was prepared for that. For a change, though, the butterflies that fluttered and danced in her stomach were friendly. They made her feel alive, and she welcomed their return.

"This one is probably going to be a little bit more [nerve-wracking] because I haven't played any matches in quite some time," she said. "But what I told myself is, 'Just go out there and do the best you can do and don't take it either way.' That's what it's all about. When I had some time to look back on my career these few years, I looked back and said, 'How many tournaments did you really enjoy and how many of them do you have memories or feelings of when you walked into the stadium?' It was like, 'Not too many.' That's one thing I'd like to change."

In Monica's voice—in her words—one could detect both strength and peace. At twenty-one years of age, she was no longer a child. She was a woman. Time and circumstance had stripped away any lingering naivete, but somehow she had retained her zest for life. It was at once refreshing and reassuring.

"It was a very tough decision to come back," Monica said. "But I love to play tennis. It is something that I love to do. I have that chance and I'm just going to go out there and try it. You're here on this earth to be happy. I will overcome what happened to me. It is time to move forward."

Chapter 12

"A SPRING RAIN"

They rolled out the red carpet in Atlantic City. Literally. It stretched from the tunnel beneath the stands at the cavernous old Convention Center all the way to center court. As she walked stride for nervous stride with Navratilova, her face locked in a tight smile, Monica Seles could hear the faint rumble of approval. She could feel the energy. And then she could see them, eleven thousand spectators standing and cheering and applauding. Some were even crying.

The ovation went on for more than two minutes, during which Monica—wearing a white dress adorned with the Nike "swoosh"— waved and giggled and smiled. But as the applause echoed off the walls, and the crowd refused to fall silent, Monica was nearly overcome by the emotion of the moment. She dipped her head into her hands, as if trying to hide. There was nowhere to run, though. And no need to run. This was where she belonged: on stage. Monica quickly gathered herself and responded to the crowd once again. She exchanged a high five with Navratilova, whose unrelenting efforts on Seles's behalf were now validated. And then, more like teammates than opponents, the two women embraced and kissed.

"Leading up to here, it's been pretty nerve-wracking, especially the last week or so," Monica would later say. "Today when I walked through the locker room and onto the court, it was just an unbelievable feeling. I can't even put it into words."

There was so much about this event that reeked of Atlantic City tackiness: the centurions in helmets who lined the red carpet (the event was sponsored by Caesar's Palace); Cleopatra throwing rose petals at Monica as she walked through the hotel lobby on the afternoon of her arrival; Caesar himself offering the warmest of greetings as she stepped onto an elevator.

All of this was to be expected. Navratilova-Seles was, at its core, a made-for-TV event designed to suck in a vast audience of curiosity-seekers. It was not a true athletic event; it was a *product.* Somehow, though, it rose above the camp and circumstance to become much more than that. For Monica, it was an opportunity to test her emotional and physical fitness in front of a live audience, and to prove to the world that she would indeed be back. For the fans at the Convention Center, it was a chance to see two great players—one at the end of a brilliant career, the other embarking on a *second* career—in a uniquely personal event.

The fact that Navratilova was thirty-eight years old and semiretired—her competitive schedule included only World TeamTennis, exhibitions, and doubles matches—did not matter in the least. That she was hampered by a nagging groin injury, which nearly forced the cancellation of her match with Seles, did not seem terribly important. She was, after all, *Martina*, arguably the greatest player in history. If she felt this was a worthwhile venture, then it probably was.

The tennis, especially in the beginning, was not particularly impressive. Obviously nervous, Seles double-faulted on the first point of the match, but came back to win the opening game on a blistering service winner—a shot as muscular as any she had ever unleashed. It was a clear indication that, at twenty-one, she had loosened herself from the grip of adolescence. Monica was undeniably rusty but also stronger.

"To me, she played as well as she did two years ago," Navratilova observed after the match. "I didn't see any gap. It was like she was in a time warp or something."

In some ways Monica actually appeared to have improved. Her serve was bigger, and she was less inclined to hug the baseline. Indeed, as the night wore on, it became apparent that the crowd was being treated to a sneak preview of the new Monica Seles. She was a work in progress, but it was fairly obvious that she planned to be a better, more versatile player. In addition to the stinging groundstrokes that had long been the most reliable part of her arsenal, she now revealed a game that included a potentially devastating serve-and-volley attack.

If there was one thing that seemed to be missing, it was the loud grunt that used to accompany Monica's every shot. Early in the match it was infrequent and barely audible. At one point in the first set a spectator even pleaded with Monica to start grunting louder. She did, too. As the match grew longer, and as she gained confidence, Monica's guttural cry increased in volume, until, on longer points, it matched the intensity of her earlier years.

"Unnnhhhh-EEE!"

Seles held serve to take a 4–3 lead in the first set, then broke Navratilova with a searing crosscourt forehand deep in the corner. Navratilova barely got a racquet on the ball. Seles had reached break point with a smooth backhand winner that prompted Navratilova to bow in admiration—and the crowd to howl in delight.

For her part, Monica could only smile.

"A lot of times," she said, "I couldn't even believe the shots I hit."

Seles held serve again to close out the first set at 6–3. As with each previous changeover, she sat in a chair with her back to the crowd, just as she had before the stabbing. Security, however, was tight. Forming a human barricade around the court were more than a hundred security guards from the Convention Center, Caesar's Palace, and the Atlantic City police force. Another layer of protection was provided by a bodyguard, who sat behind Monica.

The army neither distracted Seles nor detracted from the crowd's enjoyment. For both, it was a night to celebrate.

"The electricity of the crowd is what I missed most," Monica said. "It's great to be back."

Seles broke Navratilova to open the second set, and then broke again to take a 5–2 lead. She held serve to end the match. It was a bravura performance, and when it was over Seles and Navratilova met at the net to share another embrace as the crowd thundered its approval. If there was anything about the evening more impressive than Monica's skill with a racquet, it was Martina's style and grace. She played as hard as she could, but never lost sight of the fact that it was Monica's night. On the court and in a post-match press conference, Navratilova was practically reverential.

"Those passing shots were not a mirage," she said. "She beat me, and I ain't no slouch potato out there. I didn't play badly. Monica is going to be a contender anywhere she plays. She's playing great tennis. I didn't see much difference from when I last played her. The second point, she hit a laser passing shot down the line. She hit three winners the first game, like she hasn't missed a beat."

So, how long would it take Monica to regain her old form, and perhaps sole possession of the number-one ranking?

"Tennis-wise, she's right there," Navratilova said. "And mentally, she's always been tough. Emotionally, she handled it great today. I expect her to sail through it."

Before exiting the court, Monica accepted another long and loving round of applause. She even took microphone in hand and addressed her fans. "I just want to thank you all for your support through this time," she said. "For a long time, I didn't see light at the end of the tunnel. But, hopefully, the next few years are going to be a lot better."

Then, as she made her way to the press room, Monica did something totally unexpected— something that would have been impossible a year earlier.

She stopped.

And as the fans shoved programs and hats and T-shirts in front of her, she scrawled her name in ink. Monica signed ... and she signed ... and then she signed some more. All the while, surrounded by strangers, she never stopped smiling and talking.

"I felt very comfortable," she explained afterward. "Everybody was so nice and they all said wonderful things, so I felt totally at ease."

Perhaps, for a while anyway, her faith had been restored. If she had not exorcised the demons entirely, she had at least come to terms with them.

Toronto would be different, the skeptics said. Toronto would bring legitimate competition: five matches in six days, against a series of hungry opponents with strong, young legs. This time, sympathy would be checked at the locker room door.

Which was fine with Monica. She gave no quarter and asked for none in return. That attitude was at the root of her greatness. If she could be delightful and charming off the court, she could be ruthless between the lines. Twenty-seven months away from the game had done nothing to change her fiercely competitive nature.

She welcomed the opportunity to play a handful of "real" matches. The exhibition against Navratilova had given Monica the confidence to take another step along the comeback trail. Originally, the plan called for her to play in the Toshiba Tennis Classic in Los Angeles one week later. But foul weather in South Florida wreaked havoc with her practice schedule, and she decided to postpone her tournament debut until August 15, at the eight-hundred-thousand-dollar Canadian Open in Toronto.

In the meantime, the WTA—apparently sufficiently impressed by her performance against

Navratilova—announced that Seles would receive a wild card invitation to the year-ending WTA Tour Championships (formerly known as the Virginia Slims Championships), a tournament she had won three times prior to the stabbing. This caused a bit of a flap, since only sixteen players were included in the WTA Tour Championships draw, and seeding was based on points accumulated during tour events throughout the year; moreover, Monica's inclusion might mean another player would be bumped. Really, though, there was no choice. The WTA had already granted Seles co–number one status, and it was painfully obvious that she was still one of the game's premier players—on the court and at the box office.

"When Monica was forced to take time away from tennis, she was not just the number-one player in the world, she was also the tournament's defending champion," tournament director Ella Musolino-Alber said. "We're now looking at another first for the Championships: two, true defending champions in the same draw."

The *other* defending champion was Gabriela Sabatini, who had won the event in 1994. An indication of whether she and Seles were now on equal ground would be provided in Toronto, at the National Tennis Centre. It was there that Monica's progress would be more accurately measured.

This time there would be no red carpet. No

centurions. No rose petals.

Just tennis.

Before facing the music, though, Monica had to face the crowd. Like a rock star on tour, she strolled to center court, basking in the warmth of another standing ovation. A crowd of ten thousand saluted her with glorious chants of "Monica! Monica!" The serenade dragged on and on, with Monica waving and smiling, and her opponent, Kimberly Po, waiting patiently on the sideline. As it had been in Atlantic City, this was Monica's show.

And, as in Atlantic City, Monica wore a white dress for the occasion, with a small Nike patch near her left shoulder, indicative of the new alliance between two industry giants: Seles and Nike had reportedly come to an agreement that would pay her fifteen million dollars over the next five years. A lot of money, obviously, but if there was a reasonable chance that Monica was still the player—and personality—she had been before her exile, then it was a solid investment.

While Kimberly Po, the 133rd-ranked player in the world, may not have been the best barometer, Monica certainly looked like a champion in her opening-round match. Biting her lip, grunting, painting the lines with vicious, two-handed groundstrokes, she was as dazzling as ever. Never mind that her new outfit revealed a bit of a bulge around the tummy, or that her legs were not quite as lean as you might expect of a world-class athlete. And never mind the daisy in her hair—a bow to gentleness and tranquility that clashed with the furiously aggressive brand of tennis she played.

Superficial appearances to the contrary notwithstanding, Seles was every inch the player she had been in her first life. In time, no doubt, she would be even better. If too many trips to the kitchen had left her with some excess baggage—"That's all the bagels and pasta," she told *Newsweek*. "In my sadness I substituted food. I didn't eat bad, just lots."—she was nonetheless impressive. As Seles sliced away at poor young Kimberly Po—she needed only an hour to post a 6–0, 6–3 victory—it was impossible not to wonder what she might be capable of doing when she was truly fit. Imagine Monica six months down the road, healthy and tournament-tough. Imagine her without the midriff roll. Imagine her taut and lean.

Frightening. Absolutely frightening.

Predictably, after the match, Seles endured another press conference in which the dominant topic of conversation was not the match she had just played, but the twenty-seven months during which she had not played. Dutifully, and without any noticeable display of annoyance, she coughed up the answers again. "I worked very hard on getting over the stabbing," she said. "I told myself, 'You're a strong person. You can get through this.' I was living in the dark for a long time. Now I see the light. It's just fun to be playing again. Tennis is all I've done from such an early age. I was missing it so much that I was not the same person."

Unfortunately, any hope for an early show-down between the two number-one players in the game was dashed early—before Seles even took the court, in fact. Steffi Graf, suffering from an assortment of physical and emotional problems, was upset by twenty-seventh-ranked Amanda Coetzer, 3–6, 6–2, 7–6 (8–6) in her first-round match.

Playing on the same court that Seles would brighten just a few hours later, Graf appeared listless and distracted in losing for the first time in 1995. It was understandable, really. In addition to her chronic back ailment, Graf was troubled by the news that her grandmother was extremely ill and by the recent legal problems of her father. Peter Graf, who handled Steffi's business affairs, had been arrested on charges of tax evasion in Germany, triggering a storm of negative publicity that followed Steffi wherever she went. It was unfortunate: No sooner had she escaped the shadow of Gunther Parche than a new controversy erupted.

In Toronto, it seemed, the burden was too much for Graf to bear. She had hardly practiced at all in the weeks leading up to the tournament, and she fairly wilted in the 113-degree heat against Coetzer. By the end of the match, Graf, one of the steadiest players the game has ever known, had committed fifty-four unforced errors—more than she sometimes recorded in an entire tournament.

"I never really felt positive during the whole match," Graf said. "I didn't really find my game. I cannot always expect not to practice and then to get into a tournament and win it. And that's not something I believe in, either. I knew it would take its toll."

Graf wasn't the only marquee player to stumble in Toronto. Sanchez Vicario, slowed by a severe cold, went out in the third round; Mary Pierce, who had a touch of the flu, fell in the quarters. Meanwhile, Seles just rolled along. First, she easily defeated number nineteen Nathalie Tauziet, 6–2, 6–2. In Tauziet's opinion, the old Monica Seles had nothing on the new Monica Seles: "She takes the ball as early and hits it as hard."

Next came a 6–3, 6–2 victory over tenth-ranked Anke Huber. That set up a semifinal match with Sabatini, who proved to be no match whatsoever. In her most impressive performance to date, Seles trampled the eighth-ranked player in the world, 6–1, 6–0. In four matches she had lost only thirteen games. And her work was not only clean, it was fast, with matches lasting, on average, a little less than an hour.

The new Monica tried to have fun beyond the gates of the National Tennis Centre, too. She spent a good deal of time strolling around the streets of Toronto, shopping and sampling restaurants. When asked for an autograph, she obliged. In sum, she refused to be a prisoner. No more glass cages. No more fear. She had made a simple promise to herself, and she planned to keep it:

Enjoy life!

As long as Monica was happy and healthy, so was women's tennis. "She was the greatest player in the game when she left," NBC tennis commentator and *Boston Globe* columnist Bud Collins told *People*. "It's marvelous having her back. I think she's like a spring rain."

Monica held her emotions largely in check throughout the week-long tournament. Until Sunday, that is. On Sunday she met the upstart Coetzer in the final, and it was as much of a mismatch as any of Seles's previous four matches. Coetzer, a diminutive (five-foot-two) South African, reached the final with victories over Graf, Pierce, and number-four Jana Novotna. But any confidence she may have acquired during that impressive run quickly melted in the sweltering heat as Seles rolled to a 6–0, 6–1 victory.

"I didn't feel intimidated by the hype around Monica," Coetzer noted afterward. "She just didn't allow me to play my game. She doesn't give you a lot of time. You have to get used to how fast the ball comes at you. You get to a point where you're confused. I wasn't sure what to do."

During one embarrassingly lopsided stretch,

Seles won eighteen consecutive games. The match was over in a scant fifty-one minutes. Court time for the week was four hours, forty-one minutes, an average of 56.4 minutes per match. She played a grand total of seventy-four games in five matches—a new tournament record for fewest games played by a champion.

Shortly thereafter Monica stood at center court, holding the winner's trophy aloft and flashing one of the most infectious smiles in tennis history. Above her, in the stands, banners were unfurled bearing such affectionate messages as MONICA—THE REAL NO. 1. As one leather-lunged fan shouted, "It was worth the wait, Monica!" the tears welled in her eyes. She fought to maintain control, but in the end gave in to her emotions.

"I can't believe this is real," Monica told the crowd. "I just feel unbelievable, being back playing tennis again, being happy and doing something that I love so much. For a long time I wasn't sure if I'd be back playing tennis again. I hope you'll understand how much this tournament meant to me."

They did. They also understood how much it meant to the game of tennis. Here was a comeback that only the coldest of hearts could not find enthralling. Indeed, it was an interesting coincidence that Monica won the Canadian Open just a few hours after another celebrated champion made a triumphant return to his chosen arena. On Saturday night in Las Vegas, former heavyweight champion Mike Tyson, back in the ring after serving three years in a federal penitentiary for rape, also began his comeback with a convincing victory.

But Tyson's return was hardly uplifting. He had expressed no regret over his transgressions, and had chosen for his first opponent a ridiculously overmatched journeyman named Peter McNeeley. The fight ended in the first round, with McNeeley's trainer throwing in the towel after he had taken precisely one punch—and not a very heavy one at that. For his eighty-nine seconds of work, Tyson received twenty-five million dollars.

A heartwarming affair it was not.

The story of Monica Seles, on the other hand, was becoming more fascinating with each passing day. And there was no shortage of pundits and scribes eager to compare her resurgence to that of Tyson's—and even to Michael Jordan's. Columnist Gare Joyce of the *Toronto Globe and Mail* said Monica's comeback "might be the one against which all will be measured." And, he opined, "Only a bloodless wretch could not have rooted for Seles. She was nothing less than the anti-Tyson."

This, of course, was another way of saying that Monica was that rarest of commodities: a legitimately inspiring professional athlete. In deeds and words she unabashedly proclaimed her love for the sport, and in overcoming such a traumatic episode, she exhibited truly heroic characteristics.

Notice had been served. *Monica was back!* And as she had in a previous incarnation, she transcended the game of tennis.

Chapter 13

THE U.S. OPEN

After her victory in Toronto, Monica was so euphoric that she boarded the wrong plane upon arriving at the airport. Not until she was taxiing down the runway, about to take off on a flight bound for *Boston*, did she realize her mistake. Fortunately, the crew sympathized, and soon she was on her way back to the gate. Given a second chance, she found the right plane and within a few hours was home in Sarasota.

With the U.S. Open one week away, Monica was advised to rest. She had discovered that even though her groundstrokes were as deadly as ever and her court sense was impeccable, her body would need time to adjust to the rigors of competitive tennis. The main problem was a case of tendinitis in her left knee, which was bound to be exacerbated by two weeks of pounding on the hard courts of Flushing Meadow. For now, though, it seemed a small price to pay. Monica returned to Florida because that was home. Really, though, she wanted nothing more than to get to New York—as quickly as possible. As she had been a few years earlier, she was thrilled about the prospect of playing in the U.S. Open. Noise and congestion and distractions notwithstanding, she loved the tournament. In the previous two and a half years, she had missed the Open more than any other event, and she couldn't wait to get back.

In a very real sense, she was the defending champion. She had won the Open in 1991 and 1992, before Gunther Parche invaded her world. Now, he was gone, exiled after so many months to some black hole of her memory. He was free to walk the streets; he had escaped justice. But he no longer held sway over the life of Monica Seles. If further proof of her recovery was needed, she would provide it in New York.

On the afternoon of Friday, August 25, a few days before the start of the U.S. Open, Monica practiced on the stadium court. It was a spirited session with Jimmy Arias, during which cameras clicked and whirred, lightbulbs flashed, and autograph hounds begged for a moment of her time. Far from being intimidated by the attention, Monica seemed to revel in it. She smiled and waved and laughed. She flipped her racquet upside down and pretended to strum the strings—an homage to her new hero, Hendrix, perhaps? She chatted with the crowd and signed until her hand began to cramp. And, oh yes, one other thing: She got in a pretty good workout, one that left Arias gasping for breath.

Later that night, after visiting a favorite restaurant, Monica came to the realization that her first day in New York had been nearly perfect. She had vowed to enjoy the game—and the life—this time around. No more hiding out in hotels. No more sleeping in the players' lounge. Each trip to a new city was a chance to explore, to soak up the atmosphere and the culture. Clearly, she was off to a good start. In fact, even though the tournament had not yet begun, the trip was already an unqualified success.

"It was very weird to be back in the stadium," Monica explained to *The New York Times*. "I felt like it was the first time. Maybe that's what this means, a new start."

On the eve of the tournament, the focus, not surprisingly, was on the top two seeds: Steffi Graf and Monica Seles. They sat at opposite ends of the women's bracket, six matches away from a stadium-court showdown on the final Saturday of the tournament. If the thought of a Seles-Graf championship was enough to make a tennis fan giddy with anticipation, it was nevertheless unlikely. For both, it seemed, there was simply too much to overcome.

Physically, neither player was at full strength: Seles had an aching knee, a problem compounded by the fact that she was still a good ten pounds overweight; Graf had bone spurs in her back and left foot. Moreover, both players were trying to cope with emotional stress: Seles's stemmed, of course, from her prolonged absence; Graf's was the result of her father's ongoing legal problems. While Steffi tried to concentrate on tennis, images of her father, locked away in a German prison cell, kept flashing in her mind's eye.

"I'm going to try and play the Open," Graf said before the tournament began. "But I honestly don't think it's possible for me to concentrate one hundred percent on tennis right now."

Monica was similarly cautious in assessing her chances. "To be realistic about it, it's going to be pretty hard to win the Open after being so long away," she said. "But hey, you never know."

True enough. On Monday evening, beneath a clear, moonlit sky, Monica walked onto the Stadium Court. Predictably, and appropriately, the crowd stood as one and showered her with applause. Monica, who appeared completely at ease, waved appreciatively. Then she got down to business. With a dazzling array of ground-strokes, drop shots, spins, and slices, she thoroughly overwhelmed her first-round opponent, Ruxandra Dragomir of Romania. The match took just fifty-six minutes. The final score was 6–3, 6–1.

When it was over, Monica dashed into the crowd to share the moment with her parents. Then she accepted a congratulatory hug from former New York mayor David Dinkins, an ac-

knowledged tennis fanatic who rarely missed the
Open.

At a post-match press conference, Seles told
reporters that she wasn't nearly as calm as she
may have looked. "I went out there just trying
to focus on the ball, and I just wasn't focusing,"
she said. "I wasn't really conscious out there. I
was so stiff."

If this was "stiff," then Dragomir could only
imagine the devastation likely to be heaped
upon the poor women who caught Seles on a
"loose" day. "I don't think Monica has any
weakness," Dragomir said. "I think she can win
this Open. I can't say if she was better before or
better now. I think she's the same."

Well, not *exactly* the same. The old Monica
would have retreated to her hotel after the
match. The new Monica opted for a few hours
of entertainment at . . . *Giants Stadium?!* Yup.
While most of her fellow players were punching
up the latest Spectravision offering in their hotel
rooms, Seles traveled to the New Jersey Mead-
owlands for the New York Giants Monday night
season opener against the Dallas Cowboys. This
was not just a one-shot deal, either. True to her
word, Monica *experienced* the Open this time.
During the New York fortnight she took in a
couple of Broadway shows, attended the MTV
Music Awards, and acquainted herself with
many of the city's finer shops.

On Wednesday night, for example, she

stopped at Barney's department store. Like a dreamy young girl out shopping for the first time, she lingered in the hat department, modeling in front of a mirror. It was, she would later recall, one of the highlights of her visit to New York—a simple pleasure that had nothing to do with tennis. "There was, like, absolutely nobody there," Monica said the next day, shortly after beating 113th-ranked Erika de Lone, 6–2, 6–1. "It was almost closing time and I'm trying on all these hats. *One hundred hats* that I can try on with nobody coming near me. Just this music playing. And it was like right out of the movies, like when you see Audrey Hepburn. I mean, like it was *wow*, it was the best."

Seles's third-round match represented a step up in competition: her opponent was twenty-eighth-ranked Yone Kamio of Japan. It also marked the first time she wore a knee brace during a match. Previously, she had used it only in practice, but now the tendinitis was flaring up, leading to speculation that a two-week tournament so early in her comeback might prove too demanding.

It didn't take long, however, for Monica to silence the skeptics. She played nearly flawless tennis against Kamio, giving up only one break point in a 6–1, 6–1 victory. Fifty-four minutes after the match had begun, it was over, and now Monica was trying to convince reporters that the emergence of the brace (actually, it wasn't really a brace, in the traditional sense of the word, but a sleeve, designed to provide warmth and a small degree of stability) was not a particularly significant development.

"My knee was sore this morning so I thought it was better to be safe," she said with a shrug. "This morning and yesterday, it hurt. I wanted to see how it felt with [the brace] on. I might just wear it until I lose."

Regardless of when that moment came, Monica wanted everyone to know that she was remaining true to her goal: She was having fun. "I can't believe that I'm actually here," she said. "I'm comfortable signing autographs. Everyone is so nice. I'm just having a great time."

The new Monica Seles was alert, aware, sensitive—less egocentric than the old Monica Seles. Time and circumstance had given her enormous perspective. Once in a while, she knew, it was appropriate to drop the shield. So it was that when Monica walked into the women's locker room prior to her fourth-round match against number eleven Anke Huber and came upon the sobbing, shaking form of a demoralized and defeated junior player named Edit Pakay, she felt compelled to offer a sturdy shoulder. Monica handed the fifteen-year-old Hungarian a handkerchief, then sat with her while she regained her composure.

If that sounds like a minor good deed, well, it really was much more. In the tense moments before a Grand Slam match, players are typically so nervous, focused, and self-absorbed that they

are oblivious to all outside activity. Just minutes
before one of the most important matches of her
life, Monica tore down that invisible wall and
reached out to someone less fortunate. It was an
extraordinary gesture of kindness.

"I saw the girl that was crying and I thought,
'Wow, I used to cry when I lost matches,' " Seles
later said. "But you shouldn't really cry over losing a tennis match. Tennis is a sport. It should
never go beyond that. I told her, 'You know, life
is not over that you lost one tennis match.' "

Not that anyone could really remember the
last time Seles lost a match. After brushing away
Pakay's tears, Monica—with each of the finger-
nails on her right hand painted a different
color—walked onto the Stadium Court and blew
away Huber, 6–1, 6–4. A moment of pre-match
tenderness had done nothing to dampen her
competitive spirit. That, of course, made the victory even sweeter. It was proof that she could be
a gentle, caring human being *and* a relentless,
fiercely competitive athlete. It was possible to
live in both worlds. For Monica, another lesson
learned.

In the quarterfinals against fourth-ranked Jana
Novotna, she had to call upon every ounce of
her renowned mental strength. Trailing 6–5,
40–15, in the first set, Seles fought off two set
points to get back to deuce. For Novotna, that
was the match. Her will had been broken.

"She didn't worry at all about what the score
was," Novotna said admiringly. "She just went

for her shots. Any other player would just put the ball back in play. I served right into her body and she was able to go for a winner down the line, which is absolutely amazing. But this is the Monica we know from the past. She hasn't lost anything of this."

Seles won the opening set, 7–6 (7–5)—"Once the first set was over, it was over for me," Novotna later conceded—and breezed through the second set, 6–2. It was by far her most difficult match of the tournament to date, but once again she was triumphant. In five matches Monica had yet to drop a set. For a rusty, slightly overweight player, she was putting on quite a show.

Of course, the demands of the role were growing with each successive match. Waiting in the semifinals was Conchita Martinez, the third-ranked player in the world. Martinez had been a bit of an underachiever early in her career, but had blossomed in recent years. She had captured her first Grand Slam title at Wimbledon in 1994, and reached the semifinals of every Grand Slam event in 1995. Clearly, her star was ascending.

And yet, for Martinez, there was an imposing mental barrier to clear: She had never beaten Seles. When reminded of this fact, Martinez's eyes turned cold: "Really, the past was past," she said. "Now we're here in the present."

As it happened, the present looked very much like the past. With characteristic precision, Monica ran Martinez ragged. With a devastating combination of power and accuracy, she played the role of puppeteer, moving her opponent from one side of the court to the other. It was an awesome sight: Seles at the baseline, teeing off, drilling a shot deep into the left corner, Martinez chasing it down, feebly returning the ball, only to have it come blazing back over the net, this time deep in the *right* corner.

And on those rare occasions when Martinez seemed on the verge of controlling a point from the baseline . . . *plop!* Seles would break her heart with a perfectly executed drop shot.

In precisely one hour Monica reaffirmed her mastery of Conchita Martinez. The final score was 6–2, 6–2. Nearly two weeks and six matches had passed since she arrived in New York, and still she had not dropped a set. Routine as the victories were becoming, it was impossible not to marvel at her performance, and no one was more bewildered than Monica.

"Everything about life is funny," she said after beating Martinez. "If you can't laugh at life, then why are you living? Just to be in the final, gosh! If someone had told me one or two years ago that I was going to be in the final here, and have a chance to go out and play great tennis tomorrow . . . it's beyond what I dreamt of."

Ah, yes . . . tomorrow. A date with destiny. For just as Seles was plowing through her half of the bracket, so too was Steffi Graf. Gabriela Sabatini had put up a noble fight in the tournament's other semifinal, but Graf had prevailed, 6–4, 7–6 (7–5), setting up one of the most dramatic and eagerly anticipated championship matches in U.S. Open history—in *tennis* history, for that matter.

Finally, after two and a half years, they would meet on opposite sides of the net. The two best players in the game. Two extraordinary athletes tethered not only by their talent, but by a single, tragic event. Number one vs. number one.

"I'm excited to be in the finals and play against her," Graf said. "No one has missed having Monica on the tour in quite the same way as I have. And no one has had the same kind of feelings about why what happened to her happened. All that ever mattered to me was that she came back to play tennis—if that was what she wanted to do."

They wanted the same thing. Now it was time for their dreams to merge.

Stefan Edberg, one of the sport's greatest players, referred to the 1995 U.S. Open as "a Seles Open." And so it seemed as she walked onto the Stadium Court Saturday afternoon. Seles and Graf matched strides as the crowd stood and cheered. And while the argument could be made that Graf had been equally courageous in reaching the final, somehow it seemed that the audience response was intended primarily for Seles.

Once the match began, however, loyalties were divided. Rarely had a match provoked such conflicting emotions. It was impossible not to root for Monica, who had endured so much, and whose comeback had been so inspirational. At the same time, how could anyone not feel for Graf, whose body and soul ached? She was, arguably, the greatest player of her time, a winner of seventeen Grand Slam titles—just one fewer than Navratilova and Evert. Moreover, and perhaps more importantly, she was a class act, gracious in both victory and defeat.

But there could be only one champion on this day. The best the crowd could hope for was a long and thrilling match, two hours of brilliant tennis in which each competitor had her moment of glory, if not her moment of victory.

The first set lived up to expectations. In breathtaking fashion, the two players hammered at each other, trading games until the score reached 6–6. Appropriately enough, a tiebreaker would be required to decide the opening set. For Seles, this was not a bad thing. The tension inherent in a tiebreaker prompted some players to wilt; it seemed to bring out the best in Monica. And, true to form, she took a 6–5 lead in the tiebreaker and had an opportunity to serve for the set.

Monica rocked back, tossed the ball high, and unleashed a powerful serve down the middle. The placement was nearly perfect. Graf had no chance. The ball kissed the line and bounced high into the backstop.

Ace!

Seles smiled, pumped her fist, and jogged toward the sideline, certain she had won the set;

sure she was halfway to victory. After only a few steps, though, she was stopped dead in her tracks by the sound of the linesman's late—and questionable—call. The serve, he said, was wide. Monica pleaded with the umpire, but he refused to overrule the linesman. Graf then jumped on Seles's weak second serve, smacking a forehand winner crosscourt to tie the score at 6–6.

Usually the coolest of customers, Monica was still steaming and arguing with the umpire when she went to the end line to await Graf's serve. Her concentration broken, Monica committed two consecutive unforced errors to lose the tiebreaker and the set.

During the changeover, a beefy bodyguard stood behind Monica's chair—the only visible remnant of the incident that linked the two champions. But it was not his presence that distracted Seles, it was the linesman's call.

"I thought about it too long," Monica said. "I was reminiscing so much about that one serve. Two and a half years ago, if I have that call, I would say, 'O.K., Monica, it's gone.' This year it was bugging me through the whole match."

A single call did not determine the outcome of the match, however. If anything, Seles's competitive fire was stoked by what happened in the tiebreaker. For in the second set she was nothing short of awesome, blanking a surprisingly nervous and tentative Graf, 6–0. It was the first time in twelve U.S. Open appearances that Graf had lost a set at love, and it was the first time since the 1992 French Open semifinal (against Arantxa Sanchez Vicario) that she had lost a set at love in a Grand Slam tournament.

In addition to suffering from a case of the jitters, Graf was hampered by the bone spur in her left foot. But after the first game of the third set she changed her bandage and socks, and from that moment on, Graf seemed to be more fluid and comfortable. The nervousness, too, faded.

And, inevitably, Monica began to tire. It was bound to happen. After so many matches in such a short period of time, her body stopped listening to her mind. No one on the women's tour is tougher than Monica Seles; no one has a greater will to win. But the fact remained: She was playing in just her second tournament in twenty-eight months. She was not sharp and she was not in shape. She had been surviving on strength and skill, not stamina. Now, as the unforced errors began to mount, and as she double-faulted to give Graf a 3–1 lead in the third set, it was clear that the tank was finally running dry.

But the end was not without high drama. Serving at 5–4 in the third set, Graf took a 40–15 lead. Double match point. Graf's first serve tickled the net and sailed long. The crowd gasped. On the second serve, Seles, gutsy to the end, ripped a two-fisted backhand winner crosscourt, deep into the corner. For a moment, the crowd reacted with stunned silence, as if struck dumb by the power of the shot, and the confidence required to deliver it under such tense circumstances.

And then . . . a roar of appreciation and approval. Please continue, they seemed to be saying. *Please . . .*

In a heartbeat, though, it was over. Another serve at match point—this one clean—a forehand return by Seles into the net, a cry of joy and relief from Graf. And then . . . a moment of absolute magic. As the crowd stood and saluted the two graceful warriors, they came together at the net and buried the past once and for all. For an instance, as their arms reached out, they painted a tender, yet confusing picture. On Steffi Graf's face was a look of anguish; on Monica's was a smile. They embraced, kissed. And one wondered . . . *who was the winner?*

Even in the press room, during post-match interviews, it was difficult to tell who was happier.

"This is the biggest one I have ever achieved," Graf said. "Nothing can ever come close to this one. I had a lot of obstacles to climb over, and a lot of things that were difficult to focus on, because every time something else was coming up."

And it kept coming up even now, intruding on her moment of triumph. In the bowels of the National Tennis Center, in front of hundreds of reporters and television cameras, Steffi Graf was asked if she would have an opportunity to speak with her father about her victory in New York. "I don't think so," Graf said. Then, suddenly overcome with emotion, she stopped talking. She covered her face with her hands and fled the press room, sobbing uncontrollably.

In contrast, Monica was practically jubilant, despite the loss. "It has been very exciting to me playing again," she said between giggles. "Just being out there, feeling everything again. As long as I keep having fun, that is what is going to matter to me the most."

Monica was careful to mention her respect and admiration for Graf, just as Graf had complimented her. And there was nothing false about it. On a bright and beautiful New York afternoon, they had brought out the best in each other, and in so doing, they had given the game one of its finest days.

Best of all, they had made it clear that this was not the end; rather, it was a new beginning.

"We both hit the ball hard," Monica said. "Whenever we play again—and we will—I'm sure it's always going to be strong tennis."

She smiled as she spoke, a champion even in defeat. Already Monica was thinking about the future, preparing for it, reaching for it, dreaming of it.

Like her father always said . . . *move on.*

Epilogue

THUNDER DOWN UNDER

Shortly after the U.S. Open, the Monica Seles Comeback Express was derailed. Apparently, the shock of world-class competition was more than her body could withstand. Adrenaline and courage had sustained Monica in Flushing Meadow, but when the excitement wore off and she assessed her physical condition, the prognosis was not good. The tendinitis in her knee would dissipate only with rest and rehabilitation. The same was true of her chronically sore ankle.

So Monica returned to the sidelines. Throughout the fall of 1995, she repeatedly withdrew from tournaments. As her tendons and ligaments were healing, though, the rest of her body was weakening. It was a terrible cycle: In order to achieve peak fitness, Monica had to train feverishly; but until she was healthy, she could barely train at all. After so much time away from the game, and after mounting such a wonderful comeback, she couldn't bear the thought of another sabbatical. Nevertheless, that was the prescription.

By November, Monica was already battling occasional bouts of depression—and the worst was yet to come. A virus left her with a case of vertigo that at times made it difficult to get out of bed. Physicians at first diagnosed her malady as meningitis; later it was determined that she merely had a nasty case of the flu.

It was several weeks before Monica felt strong enough to begin working out. By the middle of December she was hitting every day on the courts outside her home. It felt good to swing a racquet, to sweat, to run. So good, in fact, that she decided to return to competition. Monica traveled to Sydney in the second week of January to play in a tune-up for the Australian Open. Her performance there—she defeated Lindsay Davenport in the final—gave rise to optimism. Another long layoff, another championship. Now . . . if only she could stay healthy.

But luck was not with Monica. Within hours after the tournament in Sydney had concluded, her body began to rebel. By the time she played her first-round match at the Australian Open in Melbourne, she felt less like a number-one seed than a longshot. Not only was her ankle bothering her again, but she had also pulled a groin muscle. Her hip hurt, too. Worst of all, though, was her left shoulder, which—thanks to a strain incurred while lifting weights—throbbed with each shot.

Injuries and a lack of fitness (she was still overweight) seemed sure to conspire against Monica in her bid to capture her first Grand Slam title in three years. The Australian Open had always been one of her favorite tournaments. She had been champion in '91, '92, and '93, and she wanted nothing more than to reclaim her crown. A week earlier that had seemed an attainable goal, especially with Steffi Graf out of the picture. Graf, who was recovering from foot surgery, had withdrawn from the Australian Open, leaving Seles as the favorite. As the tournament progressed, however, it was clear that Monica was in distress. She tired easily. Her strokes were neither as accurate nor as sharp as they had been at the U.S. Open. Despite daily doses of physical therapy and massage, she was in almost constant pain.

Still, her competitive fire would not be doused. In a semifinal match against nineteen-year-old Chanda Rubin, one of the tour's most promising young players, Seles found herself in a deep hole. Rubin took a 5–2 lead in the third set and was within two points of winning the match. As she had done so often in the past, though, Monica fought back. She won five consecutive games, breaking Rubin twice along the way. When the match ended, Seles had a (6–7), 7–2, 6–1, 7–5 victory, and a place in the Australian Open final.

That match turned out to be a far less dramatic

affair. Huber broke Seles to take a 3–2 lead in the first set, only to have the favor returned in the next game. Monica went on to win the set 6–4, and then cruised to a 6–1 victory in the second set. After the final point, the crowd of 14,879 stood and saluted Monica with a thunderous ovation: not just applause, but raucous, heartfelt cheering. In the stands, Karolj Seles tried to wave to his only daughter, his little girl, but the emotion of the moment was too much for him. He put a hand over his face and began to weep.

A few minutes later the champion accepted her ninth Grand Slam trophy. She held it high and smiled broadly, and for a moment it was almost as if she had never left.

The truth, though, was something else. Three years had passed since Monica's last appearance in Melbourne. So much had happened. So much had changed. And yet, here she was, back on the winner's stand. Back where she belonged. She looked out over the sun-drenched crowd and smiled. The stadium fell silent as she began to speak. "It's just great to be back," Monica said in a thin, tremulous voice. And then she paused. She looked around and laughed nervously before adding, "I still can't believe I'm here."

Later, in a scene sadly reminiscent of Graf's press conference at the U.S. Open, Monica was reduced to tears by a reporter's question.

"Are you going to play any tournaments in Germany?" she was asked. Monica thought for a moment, thought about the possibility of returning to the site of her attack, of confronting those demons. Her expression changed. Her smile faded. "I don't think so," she said.

But that was not the end of it. The questions persisted. "Monica, would that complete your recovery, to go back to Germany?" another reporter asked.

"I don't know," Monica said. "I mean, whatever happened there has not been fair. I don't want to think about that." And suddenly she was crying. She tugged at the brim of her baseball cap, tried to cover her eyes. "Please," she said. "Don't take pictures of this."

But the cameras clicked and whirred. The lights flashed. For Monica, it was just too much to endure. She was too emotional, too tired . . . too vulnerable. She stood up and rushed out of the room. Within minutes she had left the grounds of the Flinders Park tennis complex, accompanied by her parents. The silver championship trophy was left behind.

It was, of course, only a temporary setback. The trophy was delivered later that evening, and within a few days Monica was playing again. Not surprising, really. She was nothing if not resilient. As men's Australian Open champion Boris Becker affectionately and respectfully noted after watching Monica's courageous two-week stand in Melbourne . . .

"She's a tough cookie."

CAREER HIGHLIGHTS

1989—Semifinalist, French Open; *Tennis* magazine/Rolex Watch "Rookie of the Year"

1990—Winner, French Open; Winner, Virginia Slims Championships; WTA "Most Improved Player"

1991—Winner, Australian Open; Winner, French Open; Winner, U.S. Open; Winner, Virginia Slims Championships; WTA "Player of the Year"; Associated Press "Female Athlete of the Year"; Youngest player ever to achieve number-one ranking (seventeen years, three months, nine days)

1992—Winner, Australian Open; Winner, French Open; Winner, U.S. Open; Winner, Virginia Slims Championships; Finalist, Wimbledon; WTA "Player of the Year"; Associated Press "Female Athlete of the Year"

1993—Winner, Australian Open

1995—Winner, Canadian Open; Finalist, U.S. Open

1996—Winner, Australian Open

ABOUT THE AUTHOR

Joe Layden is the award-winning former executive sports editor and columnist for the Albany (N.Y.) *Times Union*. His work has been honored by the Associated Press Sports Editors, the New York State Associated Press Association, the New York State Sportswriters Association, the Hearst Newspaper Group, and the Thoroughbred Racing Association.

Mr. Layden is the author of several books, including *Thin Ice* (Pinnacle); *The History of Women in Sport — A to Z* (Facts on File); *Shaq — The Magic Strikes* (Sports Media, Inc.); *High Five* (Sports Media, Inc.); *The Great American Baseball Strike* (Millbrook Press); and a series of sports biographies for Scholastic, Inc. Also scheduled for publication in 1996 are a pair of children's books on the United States Olympic basketball team (Scholastic, Inc.).

Mr. Layden lives in Saratoga Springs, N.Y., with his wife, Sue, and daughter, Emily.

In an extraordinary book that transcends sports biography, Bob Greene takes the reader along with Jordan over two seasons with the Chicago Bulls, during glorious championship surges and trying personal moments. With rare insight, Greene reveals the person inside the icon: a man who makes millions but cannot go for a quiet walk around the block without getting mobbed, a man who competes ferociously on the court, but who performs some of his most remarkable and unexpected feats away from the limelight.

HANG TIME

BOB GREENE

"Jordan seems to open up more to Greene than anybody."
—Mike Lupica, New York *Daily News*